TENNESSEE

Territory to Statehood

Dave Foster

ISBN 0-9644613-2-3
Published by Top Tenn Press, Inc.
(865)-249-1548 or (407)-422-0455
E-mail: toptennpr@aol.com
Printed in the United States of America

0 1 2 3 4 5 6 7 8 9

This book is dedicated to my wife Joyce.
Dave Foster

Edited
By Dean Warren

Front Page Illustration
By Virginia Cherry Legge

Maps and Photos
By Dave Foster

Foreword

Tennessee had an unusual birth. Before she joined the Union the people of the area experimented with self government more than once. From Watauga to Cumberland to Franklin, the self-sufficient citizens ruled themselves, without an okay from any outside system.

This book presents part of the story. (See a Time Line of major events at Appendix, Page 89.) Only by living through the times would a person know the problems and freedoms connected with making a new life on a 'not to friendly' frontier. We've sought to describe those times and events from 1790 to 1796, when Tennessee was known as the Southwest Territory.

Dave Foster

Contents

Maps

The Settlers

Fear and anxiety reigned on the North Carolina western frontier during the 1780 and early 90s. That state then reached westward to the Mississippi River, including all of present-day Tennessee. Except for the two clusters shown by the map below, the Indian nations controlled the area west of the Appalachian Mountains. No white people lived west of the Tennessee River's northward run across the state. Settlers would not move there until after 1800 when the Chickasaws and the United States entered several treaties. These deals would convey the Indian land title to the white government.

White settlers moved onto land at the northeast tip and center section of today's Tennessee, starting after the mid 1760's. They had either leased or bought the rights from the Cherokees.

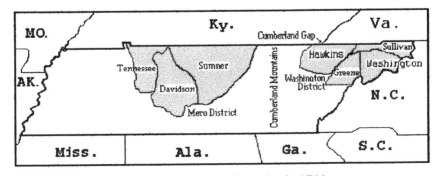

North Carolina Western Counties in 1790

Several main citizens came to the eastern sections early. The people and their areas were: Evan Shelby, north of Holston

Fear and Anxiety Reigned

River's Long Island; Valentine and John Sevier, Watauga; John Carter, Carter's Valley; and Jacob Brown, Nolichucky. All the land these settlers claimed fell within the later-to-be Washington and Sullivan Counties.

Many early families moved from Washington District to the Cumberland River Valley, which was later to become the Mero District. During the winter of 1779-80, under the leadership of James Robertson and John Donaldson, these pioneers relocated to present-day Middle Tennessee. Robertson led the adult males of these families. They loaded their belongings on wagons and herded their farm animals along the land route. They passed through the Cumberland Gap to the Cumberland Valley.

At the same time, John Donaldson led the women and children on a flotilla down the Tennessee River. They paddled up the Ohio River and continued up the Cumberland River. The land travelers had already arrived at French Lick (later known as Nashborough and then Nashville).

As they had done in the East, these early settlers built small forts, or stations, to protect themselves against the frequent Indian attacks. With today's modern transportation system, well-stocked stores and peaceful times, it is hard to picture the hardships these early settlers faced in their daily lives. Most settlers eked out a living by working the earth. Often one person stood guard against surprise Indian attack while others worked the land.

This new country required endless hours of tiring work to clear the trees, grub the roots and prepare the ground for planting. The newcomers planted the seed they brought to the new land.

Many Revolutionary veterans came to claim the real estate offered them for their war service. They crossed the Appalachian Mountains or traveled through the Shenandoah Valley on their trek. Most of these settled in the eastern Washington District. Some continued westward over the Cumberland Mountains and Plateau to the Mero District. This was difficult, since a wagon road between Knoxville and Nashville would not be built until 1795. Travelers to Nashville by this route would wait for a crowd to gather before entering the dangerous Indian territory. There were neither taverns nor safe houses in the wilderness.

Many braves viewed the white settlers as invaders. The Europeans and Indians looked at land through different eyes. The whites held land as an individual entitlement. The Indians viewed the land in one sense as they did the air; it belonged to everyone in common. Braves from any tribal village could take game from the communal hunting grounds. The whites protected their land titles in a court of law; the Indians protected theirs with stealth and a bloody tomahawk.

The whites, seeking a safe haven during times of alarm, often huddled for weeks in small forts. One such occasion came in April of 1793. Then a total of 280 men, women and children squeezed into and remained cloistered at Craig's compound near present-day Maryville. Several weeks were to pass before they ventured out.

In spite of these and other hardships such as danger from the natives, glowing reports appeared in newspapers as far away as London. The writer raved about the fertile country and the nearly free land there for the taking. Perhaps Governor William Blount had something to do with this publicity.

He was in Philadelphia when the Gazette published a long, hard-selling article favorable to the territory. It claimed good soil, good boat traffic waterways, good timber, and many minerals. The story said that all this made the Southwest Territory a better place to live than either Kentucky or the Northwest Territory.

Immigrants swarmed to the area. Land speculators hurried to buy up tracts from former soldiers. Many of these veterans had not seen the land, did not intend to immigrate and had not redeemed their rights.

The Holston Treaty of 1791 called for safe travel between Knoxville and Nashville. Still, anyone who moved through the wilderness had good reason to fear an attack. Even after they had safely arrived at their destination, build a cabin and planted their crops the settlers could forfeit their lives.

Governor William Blount was the Federal Government's point man and main author of the Holston Treaty. He held two jobs: Superintendent of Indians Affairs of the Southern nations as well as the territory governor.

William, born March 26, 1749, in Bertie County, North Carolina, grew up in a privileged household. His family engaged in business in a big way, selling tar, farm products and manufactured goods. They ranged over a wide area from their headquarters in Bern, North Carolina. The family had moved closer to its main markets near the Carolina coast. Currency transactions added depth to their profits. Insider information helped the family gain business, and state politics played a big part of the success in their business schemes.

William Blount

William went into Carolina politics early, serving two terms in the lower House during 1780-84. The legislature sent him to the Continental Congress for the 1783-84 and the 1786-87 terms. He reluctantly signed the new United States Constitution to make it unanimous, but said it needed more protection such as a bill of rights.

With the help of politics he made even greater business profits. He learned how to switch points of view as fast as a chameleon can change colors, an ability that assisted both business and political interests.

Examples are: He answered the royal North Carolina governor's call to help put down the regulator rebellion. Within a few months, after the Revolution had gotten under way, he joined the local militia. When he was a state legislator, he cast most of his votes along with his coastal neighbors. His land speculations called for him to sully up to the pioneers beyond the western mountains, and his vote pattern changed to favor them. He entered politics as a Federalist, but when he had trouble with Tennessee's admission to the Union, his colors changed again. Blount became a Democrat-Republican.

Several members of the Blount family worked in the business. They seemed to have a hand in transactions of all stripes. One very profitable line of business involved buying and selling the different forms of money. William Blount learned to buy goods using weak currency and selling them for hard cash.

With ideas of revolution spreading over the countryside, William joined his father in the local militia. The elder served as unit paymaster. When General George Washington called for the North Carolina 3rd Battalion to march north, William replaced his father and traveled with them as unit paymaster.

After the Revolution, William Blount saw great profits in land speculation, mainly in the western lands. These interests led him to push the Land Grab Act of 1783 through the North Carolina Assembly. This bill authorized the state to sell several million acres of western lands to all takers.

The law set a limit per person at 5,000 acres, but the Hillsboro Land Office agents failed to take a close look at the applicants. Blount and his partners acquired interests in 2,760 parcels in the family name. Edward Harris and Henry Rutherford, land agents for Blounts, recorded surveys of 116,000 acres in a 3-day period of 1788. All of it laid in the then western North Carolina. Most of this land stretched throughout today's middle and east Tennessee. The Blounts made extensive use of fake names when making purchases. Years later, the Land Fraud Commission would report to North Carolina Governor Ashe, on March 4, 1798, that they had found some 100,000 acres of forged or duplicate land warrants in Blount's accounts.

Protecting his stake in western land, Blount lobbied for and won the job to look out for North Carolina's interest at the 1785 Hopewell Treaty. More to the point, he looked after his own vast and growing land holdings. The Continental Congress, by conducting this treaty, aimed to arrange for peaceful relations with the Southern Indians. This confab brought together the main chiefs from several Indian nations. They met near present-day Seneca in northwest South Carolina. Chiefs of the Cherokee, Creek, Chickasaw and Choctaw nations signed the treaty. This formally set the boundaries between themselves and the white settlers.

Blount ran for, and won, an election to represent both coastal Pitt County and Montgomery County in today's Middle

Tennessee. The latter was then known as Tennessee County, North Carolina. Blount had never traversed the Appalachian Mountains and had never set foot in the western county that he represented. When he applying for travel and per diem expenses to and from Tennessee County, he asked for payment to cover 750 miles, both ways. The clerk refused to pay.

In 1787, the Assembly presented him with a problem. They asked William Blount to carry the North Carolina banner to both Congress and the Constitution Convention. Congress met in New York and the convention met in Philadelphia. Although Blount signed the new Constitution, he spent more time in New York than Philadelphia.

When North Carolina finally joined the Union by its okaying the Constitution, William lobbied hard to gain a seat in the federal senate. His efforts failed. Instead, the Carolina legislature named Benjamin Hawkins and Sam Johnson to the United States Senate.

Within a few months, President Washington appointed Blount Governor of the ceded area. Its long title was: The United States of America Territory South of the river Ohio.

William wrote his brother, John Gray Blount, soon after loosing his attempt to become a senator. Saying: In addition to "Being delivered from my State Enemies," Blount saw the appointment as governor itself as "Truly important to me more so in my opinion than any other gift of the President... the Salary is handsome, and my Western lands had become so great an object to me that it had become absolutely necessary that I should go to the Western country, to secure them and perhaps my presence might have enhanced their value -- I am sure my present appointment will."

Early in 1790, Blount sold his Georgia land holdings to concentrate on real estate in the territory. He had showered political favors on certain people there, from whom he would receive business support. One of these, James Robertson, helped Blount accumulated the near worthless congressional paper notes. The notes were "not worth a continental," but Blount had insider advance knowledge that the government would redeem the notes with good money.

His politics had helped Blount make several friends in the West. He had aided James Robertson's father Elijah, to push a bill through the North Carolina Assembly that set up the city of Nashville. He saw to it that Elijah would gain rights to 960 acre of western land. Later, James Robertson would help Blount acquire pre-redemption rights to Davidson County land.

He recommended James Robertson and John Sevier as militia generals and Daniel Smith as territory secretary. Stockley Donelson would become surveyor of Washington County with Blount's help. Donaldson would help the Blount brothers put together 150,000 acres between the Clinch and Holston Rivers and surveyed some 97,000 acres for the Blount accounts.

By mid 1791, the Cherokee chiefs met Governor William Blount at White's Fort, or today's Knoxville. By then, some 300 pioneer families already lived on land that the Hopewell Treaty had reserved for the Cherokees. Much of this land came from Blount's account. **(See Indian Nations map, page 12.)**

After Governor Blount concluded the treaty he decided to move the territory capital to White's Fort. He built a home and a modest office behind the home. **(See photos below.)**

Blount's Mansion as preserved today.

The Holston Treaty set an imaginary southern boundary that caused problems between the Indians and whites. The line ran from the confluence of the Tennessee River and the Little Tennessee River to Chilhowee Mountain. From the vantage point of a boat in the river, the mountain is clearly visible. The line, however, fades into the trees, hills and valleys of the wilderness. This invisible borderline failed to stop new settlers from moving to the fertile Indian lands farther to the Southwest. Two years would pass before a survey marked the boundary, but the influx of settlers seemed to ignore the line.

Governor Blount's Office

Both Indians and whites needed a natural boundary, and one was in the area. The Little River flows through the mountains just south of Chilhowee, and would make an ideal separation line between the whites and Indians. Blount would later ask the state legislature to resolve the problem by buying the land with the unsettled titles. Of course, this would have raised his fortunes at the same time.

Without a well-marked boundary, many of the newly arriving settlers found some excellent land to farm in the area. This would come at a high price. They often lost horses and goods, but that was minor compared to the occasional loss of life. During troubled times of the Indian uprisings, these families huddled within the close quarters of a fort or defense station. They lived on Indian land, even if they had bought the property from North Carolina.

The Native Americans

In the early 1770's, some 25,000 Cherokee Indians lived in about 200 villages near the southern terminal of the Appalachian Mountains. This native group controlled a vast terrain -- extending from what is now mid-Kentucky, Middle and East Tennessee, western Carolina, and into northern Georgia and Alabama. Their language had little resemblance to that of the other southern tribes; it was more akin to that of the Iroquois. The Cherokees hunted deer, turkeys and other small game, but they also planted gardens of corn, squash and beans.

The average-size town had 40 or 50, mostly circular-walled houses. The native builders would first set long poles upright in the ground. They bent and tied the poles together at the top and capped them with bark. Then, to seal the walls, they laced vines between the poles and plastered mud on the inner and outer surfaces. This made for a tight enclosure except for the door and the smoke-venting hole in the roof. A much larger council building with seven sides, one for each of the tribe's matriarchal divisions, served as the village meeting place. Inside this structure, blazed an ever-burning, sacred fire.

In 1743, when he was yet a young man, Attakullakulla joined several other Cherokee chiefs and traveled to London as guests of King George II. Also known as the Little Carpenter, he made friends with the first white settlers to cross the mountains in the mid 1760's. His son, Dragging Canoe, would take a different route.

A smallpox plague nearly devastated the Cherokee people in 1738, killing almost half the nation. Dragging Canoe, a leader who would rise to warrior stardom in his tribe was born two years later. Oldest son of Chief Attakullakulla, he arrived at about the time that the Cherokees battled the Shawnees and drove them northward out of the Cumberland Valley. **(See the map below.)** The Cherokees won that war even though some of their neighboring Creek tribes had fought with the Shawnees.

In 1763, England gained control of the West from France. This fact, coupled with the great numbers of white settlers moving west of the mountains, opened a land speculator's haven. In 1775, Richard Henderson of North Carolina headed the Transylvania

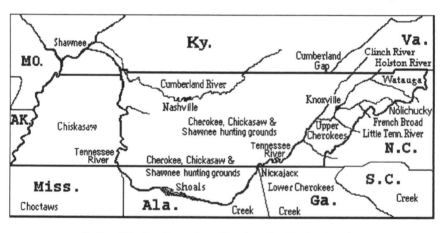

Indian Nation Locations During the Early 1790's

Land Company that closed a huge land deal with the Cherokees. The purchase also known as the 'Overhill Cherokee Treaty,' embraced some twenty million acres, the largest-ever private land deal in America. It embraced most of present-day Kentucky plus the Cumberland River Basin in Tennessee. Henderson bought this vast area. He paid six wagon loads of goods and 2,000 pounds of silver. He also gained from the Cherokees an okay for the early settlers to live peacefully. Most of these people lived near the Watauga River. **(See Map on previous page.)**

The state of Virginia quashed the Kentucky portion of the Transylvania Company land deal. Henderson lost out. In exchange for his loss of the Cumberland Valley area, North Carolina gave him a clear title to 190,000 acres in the Powell River Valley. Much of the Cumberland area went to pay war veterans. This opened a door for politicians and speculators to profit. They bought and resold many plots of land awarded to the former soldiers.

Although the Cherokees had sold the land, no one native tribe owned the twenty million acres of the 'Overhill Cherokee Treaty' purchase. Four Indian nations shared it as a giant hunting reserve.

Dragging Canoe was among those leaders present at this 'Overhill Treaty' at Sycamore Shoals on the Watauga River. In 1775, he was the young chief of Malaqua, an island town in the Little Tennessee River. Today the former island lies beneath the waters of TVA's Tellico dam.

At the title-closing conference, Dragging Canoe said: "The whites have bought a bloody land. Such treaties may be all right for men who are too old to hunt or fight. As for me, I have my young warriors about me. We will have our lands."

During the Revolution, a team of Shawnee visited Chief Dragging Canoe and persuaded him to join the British. Chiefs Raven and Abram also led their people in assaults on the settlers, but most other Cherokee leaders did not agree with these attacks. Nancy Ward, "Beloved Woman of the Cherokee," sent word to the white settlers that braves were on the warpath. Oconostota, the ranking Cherokee leader, and militia leader Colonel William Christian offered a 100-pound reward for the head of Dragging Canoe or the British agent, Alexander Cameron.

The Cherokees who joined the British efforts fought mostly during the Georgia campaign. In September of 1776, Colonel

Christian led a North Carolina and Virginia militia unit of 2,000 men on a reprisal raid and sacked 36 Cherokee towns. The victors quickly set up a slave auction and sold the captured women and children. This raid alarmed the Cherokee Nation. Under threat of the loaded gun, on June 20, 1777, they signed a peace treaty at Long Island on the Holston River.

After this treaty, more and more whites marched deeper and deeper onto the unused fertile land that the Indians still claimed. During the war, many Cherokees had moved further south ahead of this migration of white settlers. This left a large vacant buffer south of the French Broad River. **(See the map on page 17.)**

Chief Dragging Canoe, refusing to surrender to the whites, moved his people to Chickamauga Creek. This was near today's Chattanooga on the Tennessee River. Among the towns they settled are: Running Water, Chickamauga, Crow Town and Nickajack. All were located south of the Tennessee River. After a few Shawnee, Creek and others of mixed blood joined the Cherokees, the group assumed the name of the nearby creek, Chickamauga. They also went by the name of Lower Cherokees, while the Upper Cherokee towns were closer to Knoxville. The Creek natives outnumbered the Cherokees, but the latter lived closer to the ever growing numbers of white pioneers.

The Chickamaugans and Creeks, encouraged by the English, renewed the raids against the Cumberland settlers during the Revolution. In 1792, Little Turkey was the main Cherokee Chief. Due to this conduct by the Chickamaugans, he excluded them from the main Cherokee tribal doings.

After Evan Shelby and John Sevier sacked eleven Lower Cherokee towns near Chattanooga in 1779, a group of Shawnees arrived to assess the Cherokee spirit. Dragging Canoe condensed his address to five words -- "We are not yet conquered."

The group of visiting Shawnees included the widowed mother of the then young boy, Tecumseh, and his older triplet brothers. One of the triplets would die during an attack on the

Nashville area settlers.   Another would earn the name of "The Prophet."

Indian lore states he predicted a long series of powerful earth quakes. The Prophet said he would stamp his feet as a sign calling the Indians to attack and remove the whites from their land. The quakes struck between December 1811 and February 1812, shaking the earth with such fury that the land sank. The Mississippi River reversed its course and flowed backward to fill the new Reelfoot Lake, making the largest fresh water lake in Tennessee. Indian warfare on the western frontier picked up after this. Was it coincidental?

Tecumseh would gain fame as the native leader who defeated St. Clair in the Northwest.

North Carolina still carried a huge debt from the Revolution in 1783. That year, they sold nearly four million acres of the frontier land to the public to cover the debt. This they did, even though many acres in today's East Tennessee still belonged to the Cherokees. Two years later, the U. S. Congress completed a treaty with the Cherokee, Creek, Chickasaw and Choctaw nations. This Hopewell Treaty returned a large portion of land to the Cherokees, even though settlers and land settlers and speculators had paid the state. The treaty, however, did not cover the Cumberland Basin titles that dated back to the Henderson Purchase. The four Indian nations, nonetheless, still hunted in this large space that included Middle Tennessee and Kentucky.

After England signed a peace pact with the United States in 1783, Dragging Canoe opened an account with the Spanish agents in West Florida and Louisiana. He traded hides for guns and powder. The United States and Spain both claimed the land between west Georgia and the Mississippi, although three Indian nations possessed the land.

After the war, the attacks against the whites on the Southern frontier continued as they did in the Northwest Territory. In 1789, six years after the war ended, North Carolina ceded all its western land, present day Tennessee, to the United States. As a result, the United States created the Southwest Territory as a means of governing the area that would become Tennessee.

William Blount became the governor as well as the Superintendent of Indian Affairs. Since the United States dealt with the Indian tribes on a nation to nation basis, Blount reported to Secretary of State, Thomas Jefferson.

Blount acted as North Carolina's witness at the Hopewell Treaty meeting, but he had no say as to its contents. President Washington longed for peace with these southern nations, for the small United States army was busy defending the northwest settlers. The young country could not afford a war on two fronts.

The Holston Treaty

In the fall of 1791, about a year after Blount assumed total control of the territory government, he arranged a conference with the main Cherokee chiefs. He wished for peace with the neighbor Indians. All agreed to meet at White's Fort on the Holston River. This site that would soon become Knoxville, capital of the United States Territory South of the River Ohio.

The Indians loved a ceremony, so Governor Blount staged the treaty on a grand scale. He showed up in formal uniform surrounded by advisors, observers from the neighbor states and about 100 militia troops. The visiting chiefs arrived, bringing their families in about the same numbers. The scene impressed them. They had come to the meeting fearful of loosing their land, but at the same time, resolved to hold on.

The Mero District lines set by the Hopewell Treaty changed little. **(See District map on Page 42.)** The Cherokees, however, gave up some acreage south of the Washington District. The new district boundary moved westward from the Holston to the Clinch Rivers. The new southern line would start southwest of Knoxville where the Clinch and Holston Rivers meet, and then follow the Holston to the Little Tennessee River. From that point, it then would run eastward toward Chilhowee Mountain and the North Carolina border. This moved the southern border to about 18 miles south of Knoxville. **(See the Major Rivers Map below.)**

When in a boat and looking eastward from the confluence

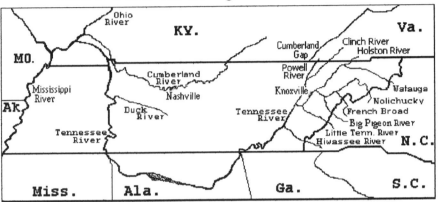

Major Rivers of the Southwest Territory

of the Holston and Little Tennessee Rivers, one can see Chilhowee Mountain. This line made a poor boundary. At other points along the new border, the many forested hills hide both the river and mountain from view. The treaty called for a survey to mark the line, and even named those from each side to run the line. The project, however, would fail to get under way until April 1796.

With no natural barrier, such as a river, this imaginary southern line was hard to control. Besides, about 4,000 whites already lived on the land south of the French Broad River, some already on Cherokee title land. Many new settlers knew the United States treaty failed to protect them, but they still located in the area.

In exchange for the goods received by the Treaty, the Indians promised the United States three things: More land, secure river traffic and safe transit along the road between the Mero and Washington Districts. This road, or trail, ran for more than 100 miles through their hunting grounds. Both the United States and Cherokee chiefs pledged to remain at peace.

Hanging Maw, John Watts, Bloody Fellow, Big Acorn and other native Americans signed the Holston Treaty. The chiefs marked the treaty paper with an X. Governor Blount and Secretary Smith signed for the Southwest Territory. Thomas Kennedy of Kentucky, Claiborne Watkins of Virginia, Tilus Ogden of North Carolina witnessed for their states.

With the treaty behind him, Governor Blount was out of the area for two months. He needed to move his family to the territory as well as conduct private business back in North Carolina. Secretary Daniel Smith acted as governor in his absence.

Before long, Cherokee tribal resentment against the Holston Treaty began to build. They observed that the United States failed to prevent new settlers from moving onto their title land. Young warriors, noting that the whites would not retaliate, increased their attacks.

The people in the Mero District suffered from raids by the Chickamaugan Cherokees. The Creeks who lived in Georgia and Alabama also renewed the raids, even though the Hopewell Treaty they signed ceded the Cumberland to the United States. Those whites who lived on Indian-claimed land felt the strongest tomahawk sting. The young braves often struck the planters on land well beyond the treaty borders.

About a year after the Holston Treaty had taken effect, the Knoxville Gazette reported a news story about Chief Big Acorn, one of the signers. He led a small group of warriors on a raid deep in Hawkins County, and murdered a woman and her child. The militia tracked the group and killed Big Acorn and his braves. Double Head, another Holston signer, met with a similar fate.

The white settlers yearned for an end to the terror of Indian attacks. So did the federal policy makers, but in November 1791, they received a bigger problem. The army, under General Arthur St. Clair, had faltered on the northwest frontier. A large, unified force of warriors, from the Chickamauga, Chippewa, Creek, Dakota, Delaware, Iroquois, Miami, Shawnee and Wynadot tribes, handed the U. S. Army a solid defeat. This ambush and battle took place near the Wabash River.

This humiliation jolted the United States and exalted all the Indian tribes, both North and South. Soon after this big Indian triumph, Dragging Canoe returned home from a visit with the New Orleans Spanish governor. That very day, a party of braves returned from Mero with scalps, and the party began. After he spent a full night dancing the scalp dance, Dragging Canoe collapsed and died at age 54.

The chiefs met and voted John Watts head war chief of the Lower Cherokees. A mixed blood, Watts lived in Northern Alabama. He was Dragging Canoe's nephew and the son-in-law of the beloved Chief Old Tassel of the Upper Cherokees. Three years earlier, the blameless Old Tassel had died at the hand of a bereaved white man who had lost his family to an Indian attack.

> # The Cherokee Nation declared war against the United States.

In September 1792, Governor Blount received word from his contacts that the Cherokee nation declared war against the United States. Watts had stepped up the attacks. On September 30, 1792, he suffered a wound while leading 500 warriors on a vicious assault at Buchanan Station south of Nashville. General James Robertson and the Mero militia, having been warned earlier, repelled the attack and held the fort. Meanwhile, a group of Upper Cherokees trod the warpath against the eastern settlers, killing some twelve people at Cavett's Station near Knoxville.

Why did the Cherokees declare war on the United States? First, their northern brothers had whipped the United States Army. Second, some 300 militia volunteers were out of the territory, having gone to the aid of General St. Clair. The victory inspired the Creeks and Cherokees and left the Southwest Territory in a weakened state.

A third reason for Cherokee anger came from a Nashville meeting of August 7-11, 1792. Governor Blount and General Andrew Pickens met with the Chickasaw and Choctaw nations. This Nashville meeting occurred some five weeks before the Cherokee war decision. When one reads between the lines of Blount's report and letters, certain facts about the meeting come to mind.

The Governor had tried without success, during the Nashville meeting, to persuade the Chickasaw nation to go to war against the Cherokees. This, the Cherokees knew. A few of their braves came to the Nashville meeting, having barged the goodwill items the United States gave to the Chickasaw and Choctaw nations. The Cherokees most likely returned home with news of the Blount's attempt to foster a war between the tribes. Some five weeks later -- enough time for the Cherokees to marshal their forces after the Nashville meeting -- Blount had an Indian war on his hands.

Governor Blount, so it seems, must have thought a Chickasaw and Cherokee war would give some relief to the killing and stealing of horses. Many of the lengthy letters he wrote to the nation's capital named the latest whites who met their death at the business end of a tomahawk. Secretary of War Knox had promised to send federal troops to aid Governor Blount, but they never arrived. After the Revolution, the public looked with disdain on a standing army and saw it as a deadly threat to the new democracy. Besides, most of the small American army was still busy in the Northwest.

The Chickasaws, led by Chief Piomingo, had befriended the Cumberland whites of the Mero District. These settlers enjoyed peace with his tribe because very few whites had moved onto the Chickasaw lands -- those lying between the Mississippi and Tennessee Rivers.

General Pickins, United States Army southern commander, had joined the governor in the Nashville meeting to recruit more

Chickasaw braves. He needed their help fighting against the northern Indians. A few Chickasaws had joined the United States effort under General St. Clair, and bad blood flared between them and other southern tribes. The split cast the Chickasaws against the Chickamaugan Cherokees and the Creeks. The Creeks, egged on by the Spanish, kept up the pressure on the Mero settlers. The Creek braves passed along the warpath through the Lower Cherokee land to raid the Mero whites. Some Cherokees joined these forays.

More than a hundred Indians, most from the Chickasaw nation, had attended the Nashville meeting with Blount. Few Choctaws attended. Several people of white and mixed-blood came to support the aims of the New Orleans Spanish Governor. From the seat in New Orleans, the Spanish controlled the Gulf of Mexico's entire northern coast as well as all the Mississippi River traffic. They enjoyed a broad trade with the Creek, Cherokee and Choctaw nations, commercial links they did not want to lose.

Some of these people circulated among the tribes to fester mischief and intrigue between them and the settlers. Militia Captain David Smith, who spoke the Choctaw language, told Blount that the red ink used in the letter to invite that tribe had caused trouble. Smith reported to Blount that a Mr. Brassheart, who looked after the Spanish interest, had told the Choctaw chiefs the red ink on the invitation was an omen. He said the United States meant to shed their blood.

Blount, reporting this story to Knox, denied he had used red ink. He wrote that Brassheart had the opportunity, and had used the color to caused trouble at Spain's behest.

Spain encouraged the Indians to force the white settlers from the frontier land that they claimed. Blount reported that this sabotage caused many Choctaws to stay away. He had received a report, none the less, that the tribe would join the whites if they went to war.

It's hard to believe that George Washington or Thomas Jefferson would sanction anything but peace between the Southern tribes. The president kept a status book on the dealings with the various Indian nations. His reference to the meeting Blount had with the Chickasaws and Choctaws shows that: 'Nothing important happened, these tribes simply wanted more agriculture tools.' This suggests that Blount worked his plan, absent instructions from the nation's capital.

The United States agent to the Creeks sent a conflicting report about the war declaration to the nation's capital. He said the Cherokees and Creeks wanted peace. Governor Blount sent word to General Robertson of Mero to reverse the militia call, but Robertson had received solid information of a planned attack.

Apparently confused by these mixed signals, Secretary Knox wrote to Governor Blount, asking him to explain the alleged and actual causes of the Indian violent behavior. Blount replied that an Indian brave could gain fame and respect by drawing the blood of the tribe's enemy. They were not currently at war with other tribes, and looked upon all white people as their foes.

In a letter of November 8, 1792, Blount gave Knox more tidbits about the Indian cultural and customs. First: Their tribal governments were too weak to restrain or punish offenders. He also described how Indian law divided the people into clans. Each clan must protect itself from harm and take satisfaction against any injury done by another clan. After this satisfaction, all would be well with both clans.

The governor relayed a story to illustrate some of the Indian teaching that "All honors come from spilling blood."

He wrote: "Chief Bloody Fellow's brother had slain a white man. Cameron, the British superintendent, demanded the killer and had him executed. Soon, Bloody Fellow murdered the Indian who had delivered his brother to Cameron, and thereby laid the matter to rest."

Secretary Knox wrote to Governor Blount, giving him an okay to defend the frontier settlers, but not to attack the Indians. The new United States Constitution, Jefferson and Knox reminded

Blount, tied the hands of a president. Congress alone held the power to declare war, but would not meet for six months. Meanwhile, the guerrilla war continued.

Washington urged all federal officers to deal with the Indians on a just basis. "They must abide by the treaties" he made a proclamation, "Or they will answer to the contrary at their peril."

Secretary Knox and President Washington, wanted to talk with the Cherokee Chiefs and asked Blount to invite them to Philadelphia. The chiefs refused the offer, but the governor himself needed to attend other business and decided to go himself. He would lobby for military help and attend to his personal business.

Governor Blount arrived at the capital when the country faced serious problems. Both France and England wanted the United States to engage on their side of the European conflict. A defiant group in west Pennsylvania challenged the rule of law and the northwest Indian tribes remained on the warpath. When placed on the stage with such profound issues, Blount and his problems gained little help from the president and secretaries.

Back home, the citizens clamored for action against the mounting Cherokee raids. During most of 1792 the Cherokees and Creeks continued their attacks, spawning fear on the frontier. This pressed the whites to clamor for reprisal.

Volunteers took up arms and raided the Indian towns. Captain John Beard led such an attack on the home of Hanging Maw, wounding the friendly chief and killing his wife. This wanton murder incensed the Upper Cherokees, as it did Secretary Knox. When he learned of this action, Knox urged Blount to place charges against Captain Beard. He did, but a friendly jury refused to convict. Later, Beard's grateful Knox County neighbors would elect him to the new territory legislature.

Governor Blount followed the United States policy line, at least in his official letters and statements. This caused the people to wonder why they must support a government that failed to solve the most important problem -- defense of their lives and property. The territory House wrote a letter to Congress stating their losses and asking for help. They named some 200 men, women and children among the killed, wounded, or kidnapped. The report valued the missing property, 374 horses and other goods the Indians had stolen, at more than $100,000.

Blount had to do something to keep his favored status with the settlers, while still towing the line on the federal Indian policy. Could he have it both ways? In concert with a few other key people, Blount designed a scheme to reduce, or end, the Indian attacks. This group included Secretary Daniel Smith, Generals John Sevier and James Robertson, and George Roulstone, editor of the Knoxville Gazette.

During the spring of 1793, when preparing a trip to the nation's capital, Blount wrote to John Sevier, saying: "If no unforeseen event takes place to prevent it and we will be at Jonesborough on Monday the 10th when and where I will be happy to meet you and we will talk all Things over." Note the capitalized Things.

A few days after the governor left Knoxville, acting Governor Smith wrote to Secretary of War Knox: "I have written to General Sevier to exert himself quickly to execute an order issued to him by Gov. Blount to have one third of the Militia of Washington District made in readiness to march for the defense of the frontiers at an hour's notice." This order must have been verbal; No written command has turned up.

Six days after meeting Sevier in Jonesborough, Blount wrote to Smith: "I presume you will order Captain Evans with his troops to the relief of Cumberland -- Your good judgment will direct you better than I can advise how far to make them or any Part of them public -- But may it not be better to keep the Contents Pretty secret let it be supposed the Order for turning out the Militia is founded on them -- General Sevier highly approves the Order and promises to enter heartily into the Measure of using it to the best Advantage -- Had you not best Immediately on the Receipt of these letters dispatch an Express to the General with Orders to hold himself in readiness to take to the field.

"He will understand the Object of, I have written him a letter from this place having in View the same Object.

"I have directed Mr. Roulstone to show the General both the Secretary's and Winchester's letters. "I had a long Talk with the General, he rode with me ten miles and may be depended upon as a Friend of Government and its officers." (I have underlined the tell-tell capitalized words.)

The word-capitalizing usage of the late 1700's offered the writer a way to more fully press an idea. Then, certain words, flagged in this manner, could stress a point as does the raised or inflected voice in today's verbal dialogue. To understand the above letters, one must study these words carefully.

Considering the flow of events that followed soon thereafter, we can make certain deductions about the letters. For example, the unauthorized marches against the Indians make these capitalized words stand out. They seem to foretell the future, or at the least show evidence of a plot between the parties.

Since Blount was out of the territory at the time, no one could accuse him of failing to follow the national policy. Several raids by volunteers, in particular the one Captain John Beard led, had enflamed both the national leaders and the Cherokees.

> # Blount was out of the Territory. No one could fault him for failing to follow the national policy.

Jefferson suggested that a federal strike against the settlers living on Indian lands would cost less than a war with the Cherokees.

Reports from throughout the Washington District proved that the Cherokees were on the warpath. This created many citizen complaints. Blount's scheming meant to soften the settler's murmurs. His ideas sparked militia campaigns against the Indians from both the Cumberland and Eastern areas.

In October of 1793, General John Sevier, the man most feared by the Cherokees, turned out a 470-man force. The militia and volunteers were from the Washington District. He planned to march west toward the Tennessee River, stay on that side and move south until across from the Lower Cherokee towns. This would calm the whites and send the Indians a message.

The Sevier force saw action almost immediately. Only a few miles west of Knoxville they met and turned back a large party. These Indians had sacked the Alexander Cavett station and killed a dozen people. The native force consisted of 700 Cherokee and 200 Creek warriors. General Sevier chased the invaders southward as they dispersed. He tracked one contingent to Etowah, a Creek village in north Georgia. After winning a fierce battle with the Cherokees and Creeks, his troops sacked the town and returned to Knoxville.

For several weeks after Sevier's attack, not a single settler felt the strike of a tomahawk, but the peace did not last. The Creeks increased their forays into the Washington District. By July of 1794, the raids had also reached a high pitch in the Mero District. Often, these small bands of Creeks and Lower Cherokees crossed the territory to strike the whites as far north as the southern part of middle Kentucky.

The Nickajack Reprisal

In the spring of 1794, Governor Blount dispatched Major James Ore of the Hawkins County militia to help defend the Mero District. Colonel John Montgomery with a group from Kentucky combined forces with Ore in Nashville.

General Robertson, Mero commander and friend of the Chickasaws, received a tip from them that a large party of Lower Cherokees had massed to cross the Tennessee. They had headed toward Nashville. General Robertson drafted plans to raid Nickajack, to which Governor Blount gave his behind-the-scene blessing.

Then Robertson issued orders to Major Ore, whose unit a number of local militia volunteers had joined. The objective was: "To defend the District against the Creeks and Cherokees of the Lower Towns, which I have receive information, is about to invade it, and also to punish such Indians as have committed recent depredations... And if you do not meet this party before you arrive at the Tennessee, you will pass it, and destroy the Lower Cherokee Towns, which must serve as a check to the expected invaders."

Joseph Brown, a first-class scout who would prove to be very helpful, had joined Ore's troupe. This young man had lived six years at Nickajack with the Indians as a slave. He knew the Lower Cherokee area well, even though he had been their prisoner.

Back in 1788, Joseph's father, Colonel James Brown, planned to move his family to the Cumberland area by way of the Tennessee River. For this purpose he built a thick-walled barge to float down the river. His wife, 5 sons, 4 daughters and five other men traveled together. A swivel gun mounted on the boat would protect them.

When they reached the Nickajack area, the Indians feigned friendship and said they only wished to trade. During the pretense they gained the upper hand, killed the colonel and either slew or made slaves of the other passengers. Chief Breath of Nickajack saved Joseph and his mother, but sent them to different towns as slaves.

Both Joseph and his mother gained their freedom in an exchange of prisoners that resulted from General Sevier's raid. While he was a slave, Joseph had learned the warpath routes used by the Indians to attack towns in the Cumberland Valley. He also studied the customs of the Nickajack people, and had seen the Creeks crossing the Tennessee River in route to the raids. The militia scouts, with Joseph's help, had already explored the area.

On September 7, 1794, Major Ore headed southeast out of Nashville with 550 mounted troops. He marched toward today's Chattanooga with support gear and supplies, including two fold-up, oxhide boats. These would help them cross the Tennessee River.

By September 12, the force arrived at the river, but had not seen the reported invaders. They waited until nightfall. Brown and two scouts swam the river and set a small fire at the river's edge. The flame would guide the troops over the dark and swollen river. With Brown's help, Major Ore moved his troops to the south bank below Nickajack, and mustered to spring a coordinated attack.

The guns and ammo had crossed in the boats in an all-night shuttle. Some troops had made rafts of logs and cane. About half the force stayed north of the Tennessee to prevent any escape across the river. At daybreak, Major Ore led the force toward Nickajack for the kill. He had divided those south of the river into a three-pronged effort. They were to attack from below, above and middle of the town.

A musket shot rang out. The premature alarm came when an Indian stepped out of his cabin into the early morning fog. The surprised native fell to the ground. Although a few troops had not moved to a good position, the surprise attack worked. Rimmed by the river and gunfire from three sides, the Indians became targets as they awoke and darted from their houses. The troops still north of the river picked off those who took to the water by boat or by swimming.

The battle ended, and 70 Nickajack warriors, including Chief Breath, lay dead. The whites captured about twenty women and children. They also reclaimed the horses and other items stolen from settlers of the Mero or Washington District.

After the battle, Major Ore rallied his troops and marched toward the town of Running Water, four miles upstream. At about mid point between the towns, the advance unit met a group of braves. These Indians had rushed to the aid of their neighbors after hearing the muskets crack.

Tall cliffs rise above the river banks, leaving only a narrow trail where the whites and Indians met. After a short-lived battle, the Cherokees saw the tide had turn against them. They fell back and faded into the brush and rough terrain. By the time the first troops reached the town of Running Water, all the women and children had fled their homes.

Major Ore set the empty town ablaze, crossed the river again and headed back toward Nashville. His attack on the bastion of Cherokee strength had cost him no lost lives and only three men wounded.

Upon hearing the news of Ore's raid, Governor Blount expressed dismay to Secretary Knox that General Robertson would order such an attack. General Robertson resigned as commander of the Mero District on October 23, 1794. Governor Blount forwarded the letter to Secretary Knox, who took no action, so Robertson retained his post.

The Cherokees knew that General Wayne had subdued the Northern Indians at Fallen Woods during that summer. The Cherokee stronghold towns were in ashes. Sensing that more white troops could soon arrive, they, along with a few Creeks, agreed to treaty with Governor Blount. On December 18, 1794, they met with him at the Tellico Blockhouse on the Little Tennessee River.

When Chief Bloody Fellow traveled to visit the national capital, President Washington had prevailed on him to change his name to Clear Sky. During peace talks, the Indians often made elegant speeches. Chief Clear Sky said at Tellico:

"I want peace that we may travel our paths, sleep in our houses, and rise in peace on both sides. I now deliver to you this firm peace talk, that our people will mind their hunting, and that both parties may rise in peace each day. My talk shall be made known throughout the Nation."

The whites and Indians exchanged captives, runaway Negro slaves and stolen horses during the talks. Afterward, several hundred wagons crossed the Cumberland Plateau without guards. The Cherokees sold venison to the white travelers along the way.

Even though Congress would refuse to pay their expenses for four years, the militia forays by General Sevier and Major Ore persuaded the Cherokees to give peace a try. Many, but not all, the tribal braves put away their tomahawks and took up hoes to farm.

Since war had fostered peaceful thoughts in the Cherokees, maybe Chickasaw-Creek strife would do the same for the Creeks. Blount and General Robertson tried to start such a war early in 1795. These tribes had already clashed a few times. One episode occurred on March 29, when the Chickasaws killed and scalped ten Creeks who were crossing the Tennessee River at Mussel Shoals.

General Robertson had told the Chickasaws that the United States would attack the Creeks. Indeed, Captain David Smith and former colonel, Kasper Mansker, led a group of Mero volunteers who marched to the aid of the Chickasaws. The troops and their cannon turned the tide of battle for the Chickasaws defending a fort on the Mississippi River.

By April 3, 1795, the Creeks were ready to talk peace with Governor Blount. Meanwhile, Chickasaw Chief Piomingo visited President Washington, who told the chief that Robertson had no authority to pledge the United States to war. The president assured the chief he would defend the Chickasaws if an European power entered the conflict.

President George Washington, Timothy Pickering, the new Secretary of War, and Governor Blount all chastised General Robertson. He resigned the second time, effective August 15, 1795. The people of Mero District, however, still loved this man who had stood between their success and failure many times.

Rare raids would continue even after Tennessee joined the Union. Valentine Sevier, the governor's brother, built a stone house at the confluence of the Cumberland and Red Rivers. He wrote the governor about an attack. The family had held on, but at a terrible cost. His twin sons died and his 12 year old daughter lost her scalp, but she would live to an old age. Valentine Sevier left the frontier, but his stone house still stands near Clarksville.

GOVERNMENT

PRE - TERRITORY

The white man learned about representative government from the Indians. Before the first settlers crossed the mountains, each Indian town sent their own delegates to their tribal council meetings. The village or clan usually chose two chiefs, one for times of war and one for peace and domestic matters. Although primitive, this was a form of republican rule.

Two years before the 1776 Declaration of Independence several early settlers formed a regime in present-day upper, northeast Tennessee called the Watauga Association. These were the first white people in America to live under a by-the-people governance. The English monarch refused to sanction this move toward democracy. He had little leverage over those of his subjects who lived so deep in the wilderness.

Until a survey had fixed the border between Virginia and North Carolina, some of the Watauga pioneers thought they lived in Washington County, Virginia. The Watauga Association petitioned North Carolina to annex them after a survey placed their land in that state. The association became Washington County, North

Carolina. On November 15, 1777, the state's new county spread westward to the Mississippi River and embraced all of today's Tennessee. Once a part of North Carolina, they elected delegates to the state assembly.

The early settlers had flirted with self rule more than once.

Other early white settlers, besides those of the Watauga area, also worked with the idea of self rule. Those people who moved to the Nashville area lived an even greater distance from the county seat and peopled centers in the East. In 1780, they formed a public union known as the Cumberland Compact. These pioneers lived in clusters around eight forts or stations, and pledged themselves to the union by a written covenant.

The settlers knew these sites as Nashborough, Gaspers, Bledsoes, Ashers, Stones River, Frelands, Eatons, and Fort Union. They elected a judge from each station much as they chose their militia leader, often the same person. As the need arose, judges from the several stations sat as a higher court to hear appeal cases.

The Cumberland Compact lasted for three years, or until August 18, 1783, when North Carolina split Washington County and set up Davidson County. The new county then sent its delegates to the state assembly.

In 1784, North Carolina had conditionally waived all claim to its lands west of the mountains. That led the settlers of present-day upper east Tennessee to set up a new state. They called it Franklin and chose John Sevier as governor. Jonesborough, the oldest town west of the mountains, was its first capital. They soon moved the capital to the town of Greeneville. The State of Franklin applied for entry into the Union, but the effort failed by a slim margin. Congress tossed the question back in North Carolina's lap.

Franklin functioned as a sovereign state for about three years, or until North Carolina reaffirmed its own right to govern. The end came in 1788 when a militia battle between the pro and con backers of the independent state settled the matter. North Carolina then took full control of the area. (Tennessee has preserved the historic battle ground, The Tipton-Haynes Site, just south of Johnson City.)

The settlers west of the mountains cried out to North Carolina for protection from the Indians. In November of 1788, the Carolina House received a petition signed by 163 people who lived south of the French Broad River. **(See Major Rivers Map on Page 36.)** Three years earlier, the United States Congress had closed a deal with four Indian nations (The Hopewell Treaty of 1785 drawn near present-day Seneca, South Carolina).

The treaty reserved certain land for Indian hunting grounds, but not before many white families had settled in the same area. They had bought the land direct from the state of North Carolina. The petitioners claimed that "The Indians gave us free liberty to live and enjoy our livings on said land peaceably and unmolested."

The settler's written statement continued: "But contrary to their agreement we suffered many injuries and losses by said Indians, which we bore without resentment. They began to murder and have actually murdered and taken seventeen persons, and finding this made no difference to the persons settled on lands claimed and sold by the state of North Carolina and those on the unappropriated lands. We were at length obliged to raise arms in our own defense or otherwise submit to the Bloody Hatchet.

"We therefore hope that you will take these matters into consideration and extend your limiting arms of protection around us, for a number of our citizens fell victim to the savage barbarity in defense of the country. Those widows and fatherless call loudly to heaven and you to consider their case and extend mercy, being reduced to so low a circumstance as to have no alternative to support their families but their small claims of land improvement, and those who have escaped their bloody fingers are reduced by loss of stock of all kinds and crops, that they must take up with hunger for their companion and familiarly shake hands with the cold hand of poverty."

The petition also asked the Assembly for permission to form a new county. They received neither help nor an okay for a new county. North Carolina's treasury was a dry well, a deep dry well. The state had issued nearly eight million dollars in bonds to help finance the war, and still owed a big debt.

Carolina's treasury was a dry well.

North Carolina failed to resolve the petitioners' problem. Instead, the state searched for a way out of both the financial and frontier political problems. The answer: give up its land claims west of the mountains, the entire present-day Tennessee. Nathan Dane, a member of Congress from Massachusetts, had proposed the solution. He said North Carolina could better protect both Indian and settler rights by ceding its western land claims to Congress. On April 2, 1790, the United States agreed to North Carolina's proposed terms and annexed the area stretching between the mountains and the Mississippi River. The nation wanted to secure its options to expand westward, checking the similar aims of the European countries.

Forests and canebrakes covered most of the wilderness land west of today's North Carolina. Although linked by trails instead of wagon roads, it lay beyond the mountains and was almost inaccessible. The distance, mountain chain and painful travel fixed a massive wall between the early white settlers and their government in the East. Both Virginia and North Carolina held claims to vast amounts of western lands, but Congress pressed them to cede these interests to the United States.

In 1787, Virginia give up control of all her land claims north of the Ohio River. This new "United States Territory North of the River Ohio" took in all of present-day Ohio, Indiana and Illinois, plus parts of other states. Congress passed a law, The Northwest

Ordinance, to govern the area until new settlers could move in and form into new states.

William Blount of North Carolina held a seat in Congress when Virginia ceded her western land. He helped write the basic law that would govern the new United States territory.

North Carolina refused to confirm the new United States Constitution of 1787 for two years. It waited for Congress to include a package of basic human rights, the first ten amendments. The state was the twelfth to join the Union, holding out until December 12, 1789. At that session North Carolina ceded the United States all its claims to the land beyond the mountains.

This, the state's second secession act, also involved a set of conditions. The terms below are in shortened form.

The people living in the new territory were to pay their share of the state's war debt. They were to pay all current accounts owed to North Carolina as well. North Carolina had covered her Revolutionary War debt by issuing bonds, and this fact accounted for the strong terms. (Little did they know then that in a short time the United States would assume all debts that the states had incurred during the war.)

North Carolina agreed that the Northwest Ordinance would also govern the territory they ceded. There was one big difference; slavery was to continue as under the then current North Carolina law.

The Northwest Ordinance required that the taxes of absentee land owners be the same as for those people who lived on a property. The new territory would honor the land titles of the land between the Tennessee and Big Pigeon Rivers and outside the then current counties. **(See Major Rivers Map on Page 36.)** Congress had 18 months to accept these terms before North Carolina would transfer sovereignty over the land to the United States.

On April 2, 1790, Congress agreed to the terms and took title to the land. They named the new province "The United States of America Territory South of the River Ohio." This did not include present-day Kentucky, only Tennessee. General usage soon cut this title to 'The Southwest Territory.' The Northwest Ordinance governed the new territory, but the basic North Carolina laws would also apply.

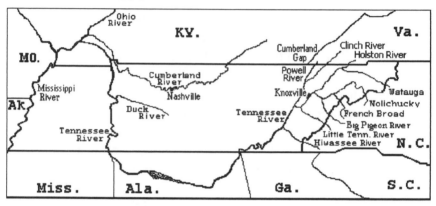

Major Tennessee Rivers

Several men, including William Blount, Joseph Martin, John Sevier and Anthony Wayne, aspired to fill the governor's chair of the new territory. President Washington named William Blount to the job.

The new ordinance armed the governor with near total power. He could do as he wished on most issues, but still had to live in the territory. Blount closed his affairs in coastal North Carolina and traveled to the frontier. He stopped to visited Carolina Governor Alexander Martin who gave him a copy of the Ordinance. Martin gave Blount a proclamation to read to the people of the new territory. Blount learned from Martin that before assuming the office he must take the oath of office from a federal official.

This caused Blount to change his route and detour by way of Alexandria, Virginia. There, he took the oath before Supreme Court Justice James Iredell, and called on George Washington. Both men had served their states at the Constitutional Convention in Philadelphia. During Blount's stay at Mount Vernon, the president made it clear that he wanted and expected peace with the Southern Indian tribes. Washington would stress this point a few days later when he issued a strong statement on the matter to all federal officers.

The new governor continued his trip, stopping by to see a longtime friend George Roulstone, owner of the Fayetteville, North Carolina Gazette. He persuaded Roulstone to move his press west of the mountains and publish the new territory's first and only newspaper. The reward for the new Knoxville Gazette would include a deal to print all the official territory papers. Roulstone first picked the town of Rogersville to locate the new Gazette, but within a year moved his paper to its permanent home at Knoxville.

The State has Preserved the Territory's First Capital

Blount chose to locate the interim capital at Rocky Mount, the estate of his longtime friend William Cobb. There it remained for over a year. (The state has preserved this historic log-cabin site a short distance north of Johnson City on Highway 19W.)

TERRITORY

On October 3, 1790, Governor Blount took his 'seat' in the governor's chair in a swift and forceful manner. He called all active North Carolina office holders of Washington County to a special meeting. The anxious crowd assembled in Jonesborough. Blount began by reading aloud the act wherein Congress accepted Carolina's terms for its release of the state's western portion.

He then read the proclamation Governor Martin had sent. It described those terms that North Carolina required in its act that turned the area over to the federal government. Next, Blount read the state's title transfer act as signed by both United States Senators, Sam Johnson and Benjamin Hawkins. He read the decree by Congress, as accepted and signed on April 2, 1790, by House Speaker, Frederick Muhlenberg, and Vice President, John Adams.

The governor paused and waved a paper in the air. He said "I have now, gentlemen, to inform you that the President of the United States of America did appoint me Governor in and over the said, Territory of the United States of America South of the River Ohio, as appears by his letter patent in the following words:

"George Washington President of the United States of America; To all who shall see these presents, Greeting.

"Know ye that reposing special trust and confidence in the patriotism, integrity and abilities of William Blount Esquire, a citizen of North Carolina, I have nominated, and by and with the advice of and consent of the Senate, do appoint him Governor in and over the territory of the said United States South of the River Ohio, and do authorize and empower him to execute and fulfill the duties of that office, according to law, and to have and to hold the said office, with all the powers privileges and emoluments the same of right appertaining, for the term of three years from the day of the date hereof, unless the President of the United States for the time being, shall be pleased sooner to revoke and terminate this commission.

"Signed: George Washington, President, and Thomas Jefferson, Secretary of State."

The next words the governor spoke must have surprised some people in the Jonesborough crowd. They came after he laid out the legal grounds that grant him such civic strength:

"From hence forward, gentlemen, all commissions issued under the authority of the State of North Carolina, to any and every person in Washington County either civil or military are void and of no effect, and all and every person will cease to act under them."

This action shows that Blount saw the Ordinance as a means of seizing total control of the territory. He used the law's stated verbiage -- "Previous to the organization of the general assembly, the governor shall appoint such magistrates and other civil officers in each county or township, as he shall find necessary for the preservation of the peace and good order in the same." Governor Blount found it necessary to replace all the existing civil and militia officers. He exercised his political prowess.

He continued the speech, saying:

"One article of the Act of Cession of the state of North Carolina is that Congress on the acceptance of the claim of territory by that act ceded, shall assume the government thereof and execute it in a manner similar to that which they support northeast of the River Ohio -- The Ordinance of Congress for the government of the territory northeast of the River Ohio, is in the words of the following."

He then read aloud the entire Northwest Ordinance. Blount had studied its words and knew its impact, for he served in Congress at its writing. A recap follows:

The statute starts by showing the high value Congress placed on land titles. It set a new standard for parceling the land titles of people who died without leaving a will.

The widow would receive one third of the personal estate, plus one third of the land for her lifetime use. All the children, and the descendants of any deceased child, were to receive in equal shares the balance of the legacy. (The oldest son would no longer inherit all of his father's land. This legislation ended this cultural theme that dated back to biblical days.)

The ordinance then details the roles of civil office holders and judges, and sets the fitness standards to occupy these offices. It called for an appointed governor, who lived in the area and owned at least 1,000 acres of land. He would serve a three-year term. A secretary, who must own at least 500 acres, would keep the official records and serve a four-year term. He sent Congress a report on a six-month basis. Three federal judges would hear the appeal cases. Each judge must have an estate of 500 acres, live in the territory, and would remain in office only during good behavior.

From the outset Blount and the judges served two functions, executive and legislative. They could pass any civil or criminal law they saw fit. Still, Congress must affirm any new decree. The governor would choose all militia officers below the rank of general. Congress reserved that chore for itself.

The Northwest Ordinance covered many issues. The governor would lay out administrative counties and judicial districts in the territory and appoint all civil officers and magistrates. He could call for a two-house legislature when he thought the time ripe, if 5,000 or more free males of full age lived in the territory. The governor, armed with the veto, could convene the assembly as he saw the need.

In order to vote, a person must own at least 50 acres. Members of the lower house would represent 300 male settlers and live in the district where he owned at least 300 acres. The house member would serve two-year terms. An upper house, to be known as the council, would consist of five members. The lower house would submit ten names to Congress, from which they would select the five-member council. The new legislature would elect one delegate to Congress. That member could debate, but had no vote.

While unveiling the solid legal grounds of his actions, Governor Blount read the long prologue plus the entire Northwest Ordinance. This reading would add more than a half hour to his talk.   He carefully laid the legal ground work for the new government and for his assuming control.

The initial Ordinance brought a number of new ideas to general governance.   To this, Congress added a few changes that predated the Constitution.   Many of these new points flowed from the pen of Thomas Jefferson.   They prescribed the freedom of worship, the rights of habeas corpus and trial by jury.   The Ordinance also ruled out the use of cruel or unusual punishment.   It forbade the taking of property except after a fair payment and mandated the government to keep out of private contracts.   It favored public schools and education.

The ordinance required the use of good faith when dealing with the Indians.   Their land was not to be taken without their consent.   Congress alone could make war with the Indian tribes.

The new territory was to spawn one or more states that would have an equal footing with the others of the United States.   The people living in the area were to enjoy both free river traffic and tax-free trade with all the current states.

The territory could join Union when it, "...Shall have 60,000 free inhabitants therein, such state shall be admitted, by its delegates, into the Congress of the United States, on an equal footing with the original States in all respects whatever, and shall be at liberty to form a republican constitution and state government: Provided, the constitution and government so to be formed, shall be republican, and in conformity to the principles contained in these articles, and, so far as it can be consistent with the general interest of the confederacy..." The law was issued before the Constitution.

After Governor Blount had read the Northwest Ordinance to the Jonesborough crowd, he laid out Washington County along its old lines.   He still had some important work left, filling all the civil and militia posts he had just vacated.   The governor named his own slate of people.

During the six-year life of the territory, from 1790 to 1796, Governor Blount would make more than a thousand of these appointments.

Governor Blount named more than 1,000 civil and militia officers.

(See Appendix A, page 55 for an alphabetical listing of the people Blount appointed to the civil and militia jobs.)

Two days after his Washington County speech the new governor traveled to the Sullivan County courthouse where the office holders under the state of North Carolina had convened. He began his talk by reviewing the same legal basis for his taking control as he had done in Jonesborough. **(See the Map Below.)**

On November 1, 1790, he gathered the Greene County officials in Greeneville and gave the same long speech. Two days later, the new governor met with the Hawkins County office holders at Rogersville. In each meeting he dismissed the county's civil and militia officers. He then appointed his own slate of people.

Within a period of only twelve days, Governor Blount had assumed total political control over the eastern part of the new territory. Using the power given him under the Northwest Ordinance, he formed all four counties into the new Washington

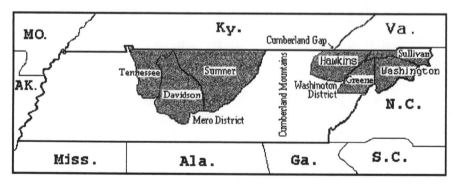

Districts and Counties of the Southwest District at its 1790 Beginning.

Judicial District. He kept the same lines of the former North Carolina judicial district.

Within a few days, protected by an escort force of 25 militia, Blount traveled some 200 miles westward. On the way to Mero District, he passed over some rough terrain. He climbed the Cumberland Mountains and crossed the plateau through the wilderness of the Indian hunting grounds.

Southwest Territory census, conducted by militia captains during July of 1791.	Free white males over 21	Free white males under 21	Free white females	All other free people	Slaves	Total, all people
Greene County	1,293	2,374	3,580	40	454	7,741
Hawkins County	1,204	1,970	2,921	68	807	6,970
Sullivan County	806	1,242	1,995	107	297	4,447
Washington County	1,009	1,792	2,524	12	535	5,872
South of French Broad	861	1,082	1,627	66	163	3,619
Washington District	**5,173**	**8,460**	**12,647**	**293**	**2,256**	**28,649**
Davidson County	639	855	1,288	18	659	3,459
Sumner County	404	582	854	8	348	2,196
Tennessee County	235	380	576	42	154	1,387
Mero District	**1,278**	**1,817**	**2,718**	**68**	**1,161**	**7,042**
Total Territory	**6,271**	**10,277**	**15,365**	**361**	**3,417**	**35,691**

Table 1

The governor had summoned all Mero District officials to a mid December 1790, meeting where they would learn about the new government. Rather than see the office holders in each of their counties, he asked that they come to Nashville. This would save him travel time.

As the meeting started, Daniel Smith presented the governor a letter signed from George Washington. The president, on Blount's bidding, had named Smith as Secretary of the United States Territory South of the River Ohio. Before he made the speech for the fifth time, the governor gave the oath of office to Secretary Smith.

He then laid out the Mero District lines as they were under North Carolina rule. The three counties involved were Davidson, Tennessee and Sumner. By the same the long speech as before, Blount launched the district, and territory, on a voyage of the new government.

In 1791, when the United States Constitution called for the first census, there was no federal money to count the settlers in the territory. Thomas Jefferson proposed that Governor Blount ask each militia captain to take the census in his area. **(Table 1 on page 43 shows the results of that count.)**

The Northwest Ordinance allowed that when the number of voters increased to 5,000 they could elect a general assembly. The militia captain's survey proved that there were enough people to elect a general assembly. An election, however, was subject to a call by the governor. Blount could have acted, but he decided that the time was not yet ripe. There wasn't a strong outcry for forming a government, and Blount suspected that a legislature would place a tax on land.

The public need for funds grew with the influx of people arriving weekly. Extra prisoners came in proportion with the added people, and that called for more jails. Many other problems required the governor's attention. The native attacks on the settlers continued. This called for action in his capacity as Superintendent of Indians for the Southern Department.

The policy makers in the capital asked that Blount set up a meeting to confer with the Cherokee chiefs. He chose to hold the meeting at James White's fort, a site on the Holston River nearer the Cherokee nation. Several white settlers lived nearby, but neither Indians nor whites controlled the area.

The governor worked with the Cherokees from September 15 to November 30, 1791. After finishing the Holston Treaty, and with George Washington's okay, Blount took a leave of absence. He wanted to bring his family to the territory, where he had decided to built his new home at White's Fort. This was to be the first two-story frame house built west of the mountains.

In March of 1792, Governor Blount laid out a town near the fort and named it Knoxville. As territory militia commander, Blount wished to please Secretary of War Henry Knox, with whom he had to deal on a regular basis. The governor also built an office on the lot behind his home. **(See photos on pages 8 and 9.)**

More and more people in search of a better life trekked to the territory. The governor had kept the six counties already in place at the Southwest Territory beginning. On March 13, 1793, he laid out Jefferson and Knox Counties and a new judicial district. The new Hamilton District would later include Blount and Sevier Counties. Tennessee County of the Mero District would divide into Montgomery and Robertson Counties and give its name to the new state. The starting six counties would grow to eleven counties before Tennessee joined the Union. **(See Map on page 47.)**

In November of 1792, the North Carolina Assembly passed a new law allowing its county clerks to raise taxes. They could charge a fee for each legal paper filed in their court. The question arose -- did this new North Carolina law apply in the territory?

Governor Blount ruled that it did not. He and the two appellate judges could, and did, use the powers to legislate granted them under the Northwest Ordinance. On November 20, 1792, the governor, in concert Judges David Campbell and Joseph Anderson, wrote a tax law.

This new measure would raise money to build or repair court houses, prisons and stocks. Some of the funds would also pay jurist costs and defray contingent expenses of the county. The highest poll tax the counties could set was fifty cents per year. The top limit on land taxes was fixed at seventeen cents per one hundred acres.

Still, if accessed to its fullest, this tax would cost Governor Blount about $1,700, that is, if all the land he owned lay in taxable counties. It did not. The Indians held title to much of the acreage he claimed.

This tax law started the settlers to murmur. After the Holston Treaty, they had enjoyed only a short lived peace with the Indians. A few rowdy braves killed the settlers and stole their horses, without redress, as the federal policy ruled out offensive action. The whites saw their situation as life under a regime who taxed them, but was either unable or unwilling to protect them.

Still, Governor Blount did not wish to change the government, and call for a territory legislature as he could under the Northwest Ordinance. As **Table 1 on page 43** shows, there were already more than 5,000 able voters living in the territory. More than a year would pass, until December 1793, before Governor Blount would call for the election of a legislature.

Governor Blount had gone to Philadelphia to discuss the Indian's war and to conduct personal business. His home state of North Carolina had named his brother a United States Senator.

One of the first things Blount did when he returned was to call for a territory assembly. He had heard opportunity knock when in the nation's capital, and this had started a march that would lead to statehood.

Governor Blount had three motives: 1. Only by becoming a state could the Tennessee people protect themselves. 2. His land speculation ideas could then go forward. And 3. He could join the Senate where his brother already held a seat. He wished to act on the statehood question and submit it to Congress before it recessed.

This was a new situation for the United States. No state had joined the Union having first been a territory. Moving toward his goal, Blount had written to ask James White, the territory agent at the nation's capital. He asked White to introduce a bill admitting Tennessee to the Union. White answered that Congress would not act, but suggested the governors ask the Assembly to call for a local referendum.

The governor could do this, and with the expected support he could call for a local constitutional convention later. A new Tennessee government would be ready when Congress got around to the admitting.

The elected members of the new house met in Knoxville on February 26, 1794. The governor stated that they were to act on only one piece of business. Their task was to nominate ten people for the Council. This the territory legislature did. They also sent a memo to Congress naming the 200 settlers whom the Indians had murdered during a three year period.

From the ten nominees named, Congress picked Stockley Donelson, Griffith Rutherford, John Sevier, Permenas Taylor, and

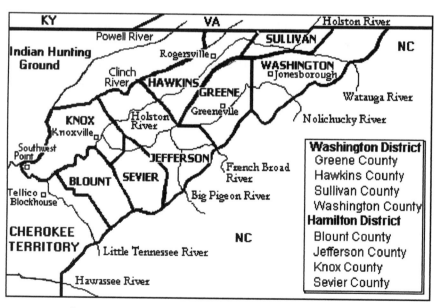

Counties in the Eastern Section at time of Statehood

James Winchester. These five would serve on the Council, or upper house of the legislature.

During August of 1794, the Assembly met for its first full working session. It limited the highest land tax rate to 12.5 cents per 100 acres. It also set up lotteries to raise funds. The legislature established Blount College, a public institution of higher learning. Years later, this college would become the University of Tennessee. That first General Assembly adjourned until the first Monday in October of 1795.

Meanwhile, given his desire for statehood, and after more input from his supporters, the governor decided to advance the meeting date. On April 25, 1795, he issued a proclamation, saying: "The public interest requires that a session of that body should commence at an earlier date." He then advanced the second Assembly's meeting from October to June 29, 1795.

The session lasted for eleven days. An appointed joint committee of two counselors and six representatives inquired into the question of a new state. The committee was evenly divided between the Eastern and Western districts. This group reported back that the Assembly should: "Take into consideration the most eligible manner of obtaining the sense of the people as to their becoming an independent state, and the necessary measures to be taken thereon."

The instructions went out. Starting September 15, 1795, the county sheriffs were to take the head count and record the popular sentiment on the statehood issue. For this they would receive $2.00 per 100 people counted. Each free male would express his wish; do you favor the territory being admitted as a state in the Federal Union, even though there are less than the required 60,000 inhabitants.

The Northwest Ordinance allowed a state to form when the territory had 60,000 settlers. The Assembly voted to start action on statehood although the feelings were not unanimous. Davidson County recorded their no vote, saying: "A change in the form of government would burden the people with additional taxes, and in taking the census, travelers may be numbered in each county they traveled through."

Thomas Hardeman of Davidson County said that the idea was unpopular, and that any census would include those who only traveling through the area. That idea would float again during the Senate debate.

Tennessee 1795 Census & Vote for Statehood.	Free, White Males Over 16	Free, White Males Under 16	Free White Females	All Other Free People	Slaves	Total Inhabitants	Favor Statehood	Do Not Favor Statehood
Blount County	585	817	1,231	-	183	2,816	476	16
Greene County	1,561	2,203	3,350	52	466	7,638	560	495
Hawkins County	2,666	3,279	4,767	147	2,172	13,331	1,651	534
Jefferson County	1,706	2,225	3,021	112	776	7,840	714	316
Knox County	2,721	2,723	3,664	100	2,365	11,573	1,100	128
Sevier County	628	1,045	1,503	273	129	3,578	261	55
Sullivan County	1,803	2,340	3,499	38	777	8,457	715	125
Washington Co.	2,013	2,578	4,311	225	978	10,105	873	145
Davidson County	728	695	1,192	6	992	3,613	96	517
Sumner County	1,382	1,595	2,316	1	1,076	6,370	-	-
Tennessee County	380	444	700	19	398	1,941	58	231
Totals	**16,179**	**19,944**	**29,554**	**973**	**10,613**	**77,264**	**6,504**	**2,562**

Table 2

Many people who had settled in the Mero District wanted their area to hold back and form its own state. The anti vote came mostly from those counties. Sumner County failed even to submit their returns.

Most voters favored statehood, with the yeas 6,504, and those against 2,562. The settlers in the eastern counties voted two to one in favor of the question. The voters wished to become a state, even if the number of settlers found were fewer than the 50,000 needed to satisfy the Northwest Ordinance demands. The county sheriffs worked for the 2 cents per person, finding a total of 77,262 inhabitants. The vote for statehood carried strongly in the Washington and Hamilton Districts. **(See Table on page 49.)**

Given the voter results, the governor called for a speedy election of a Constitutional Convention. They were to meet Knoxville on January 11, 1796. The eleven counties sending delegates were:

Blount	Davidson
Hawkins	Greene
Jefferson	Knox
Sevier	Sullivan
Sumner	Tennessee
Washington	

The Convention met in Knoxville and went to work on the constitution at once. In a matter of days a select committee came up with a new constitution. The instrument called for a new state to begin at once, before Congress gave its okay. They did not even feel compelled to submit the document to the territory people for approval.

Thomas Jefferson was the French ambassador during the writing of the United States Constitution at Philadelphia. He would have asked for stronger guarantees in that document, such as the first ten amendments. When he read the new Tennessee Constitution, he said "It is the least imperfect and most republican" of any adopted by the other 15 states.

Members of the constitution convention were the movers and shakers of the day. Most were wealthy, held a position in the territory government or both. Judges, militia leaders and populists took part in birthing the new framework of government. John Sevier, who would later serve as the governor of the state, did not stand for election to this convention. He and Blount apparently had an understanding; Blount as senator and Sevier as governor. A listing of the members follows.

William Blount served as the convention speaker, and the other members were:

John Adair	Joseph Anderson	Elisha Baker
JamesBerry	Joseph Black	Moses Brooks
Peter Bryan	Thomas Buckenham	Landon Carter
John Clack	Spencer Clack	William C. Claiborne
William Cocke	David Craig	John Crawford
George Dohorty	Edward Douglass	William Douglass
William Ford	James Ford	Samuel Frazier
John Galbreath	Richard Gammon	Samuel Glass
James Greenaway	Samuel Handly	Thomas Hardeman
Thomas Henderson	James Houston	Andrew Jackson
Thomas Johnson	Joel Lewis	Charles McClung
Joseph McMinn	John McNairy	Richard Mitchel
Alexander Outlaw	William Prince	Robert Prince
William Rankin	John Rhea	Archibald Roan
James Robertson	James Roddye	George Rutledge
David Shelby	John Shelby, Jr.	Daniel Smith
James Stuart	Leroy Taylor	John Tipton
Isaac Walton	Samuel Wear	James White

The people who lived south of the French Broad were on the minds of these new state constitution writers. **(See Map on Page 47.)** Many of these settlers had bought land from North Carolina before the later treaties had reserved the area for the Cherokee hunting grounds.

Article III states: "Until land office shall be opened, so as to enable the citizens south of the French Broad and Holston, between the rivers Tennessee and Big Pigeon, to obtain titles upon their claims of occupancy and pre-emption those who hold land by virtue of such claims, shall be eligible to serve in all capacities, where a freehold is by this constitution made requisite requirement."

On March 29, 1796, the newly elected Tennessee legislature chose by unanimous vote William Blount and William Cocke as

United States Senators. The people elected John Sevier governor over his opponent, Joseph Anderson. Governor Sevier was to receive a $750 per year salary in two installments.

The state legislators chose James Winchester as Senate Speaker, James Stuart as House Speaker, Francis A. Ramsey as Senate Clerk, and Thomas Williams as House Clerk.

Even though the new Tennessee government was afloat and active, three months of political intrigue would pass before Congress would admit her into the Union. A close national election for president was at hand in 1796. John Adams and Thomas Pickney ran as Federalist while Thomas Jefferson and Aaron Burr carried the Democrat-Republican Party's banner. Sentiment for each man on a nationwide basis was about equal, but the Tennessee settlers backed the popular Thomas Jefferson for president.

The Federalists controlled the Senate while the Democratic-Republicans held power in the House. Most people in south, including most Tennesseans, favored Jefferson in the upcoming election. This caused a big problem for the new state. The bill presented to Congress would award four electoral votes to Tennessee, one for each of the two senators and the two House members.

Several House members complained that the state constitution was in conflict with the United States Constitution. Some rivals of the entry claimed that those who favored statehood had rigged the vote by counting many people who were traveling in the area. Opponents also said that Congress alone had the power to call for a new state, not the Tennessee people. The Federalists tried another way to prevail; they claimed that two states, not one, should arise in the territory.

After the debate, the House cast its vote 43 to 30 to okay Tennessee as a new state. The Senate hesitated, playing for time on question.

Blount and Cocke presented their credentials on May 9, 1796. The Senate offered them seats on an interim basis, as spectators only, but refused to bring up the statehood bill until May 13. They debated 5 more days. Their bill called for a new census in the territory. This tactic would prevent the new state from casting its electoral votes for president. The bill to accept Tennessee passed on 12 to 11 vote.

The House refused to go along with the Senate, so the question went to a conference committee to resolve the differences between the two bills. Federalist Caleb Strong and Anti-federalist Aaron Burr served on the Senate side of the joint committee.

Blount had found a friend in Burr, and this helped a compromise to surface in the committee. Tennessee would send only one member to the House instead of two. The Senate claimed during the debate that a new member could take a seat only after having been elected by a valid state legislature. The bill came out of joint committee and passed both houses on May 31, 1796, after which, it went to the president for approval.

When President George Washington signed the bill on June 1, 1796, Tennessee became sixteenth of the United States. It was time to sew another star on the American flag.

William Blount and William Cocke would have to await their formal admission as senators until the legal new state could vote on them. When Governor Sevier received the news he called a special session of the Tennessee legislature. Again, it chose Blount and Cocke as United States Senators. The Tennessee people elected Andrew Jackson the first member to the House of Representatives.

Later that year the electoral college met in New York City. John Adams received 71 votes for President, to Jefferson's 68. Tennessee cast its three votes for the loser.

It was time to sew that Sixteenth star on the American flag.

Appendix A

Public and Military Office Holders of the
Southwest Territory from 1790 to 1796

The name spellings used in this appendix are generally the same as those shown in Governor William Blount's official Journal. On many occasions Blount limited sheriffs, deputies and tax collectors to a one year term. A person often took the same office in a newly laid-out county that he held in the former. (See James Adair below)

Date Appointed	Name	Public Office
Nov. 3, 1790	James Adair	Hawkins Co. Militia, Lieutenant
June 16, 1792	James Adair	Knox Co. Militia, Lieutenant
Nov. 3, 1790	John Adair	Hawkins Co. Justice of the Peace
June 16, 1792	John Adair	Knox Co. Justice of the Peace
Feb. 26, 1794	John Adair	Territory Assembly Counsellor Nominee
Jan. 11, 1796	John Adair	Tennessee Constitution Convention
July 11, 1795	John Adams	Washington Co. Justice of the Peace
July 8, 1795	Jesse Alexander	Jefferson Co. Militia, Ensign
Aug. 3, 1795	John Alexander	Blount Co. Calvary, Cornet
Oct. 23, 1790	William Alexander	Washington Co. Deputy Sheriff
Dec. 15, 1790	David Allison	Licensed to practice law, Territory wide
Dec. 15, 1790	David Allison	Mero District Superior Court Clerk
Nov. 1, 1790	Edwin Allison	Greene Co. Militia, Captain
Oct. 23, 1790	James Allison	Washington Co. Justice of the Peace

Oct. 25, 1790	Robert Allison	Sullivan Co. Justice of the Peace
Feb. 28, 1794	Robert Allison	Washington Co. Justice of the Peace
Nov. 3, 1790	Thomas Amis	Hawkins Co. Justice of the Peace
Mar. 5, 1792	Thomas Amis	Hawkins Co. Commissioner of Affidavits
Oct. 25, 1790	John Anderson	Sullivan Co. Justice of the Peace
July 15, 1791	Joseph Anderson	Southwest Territory Federal Judge
Jan. 11, 1796	Joseph Anderson	Tennessee Constitution Convention
Dec. 15, 1790	William Anderson	Davidson Co. Militia, Lieutenant
Sept. 24, 1793	James Armstrong	Hawkins Co. Militia, Ensign
Oct. 23, 1790	Nathaniel Armstrong	Washington Co. Militia, Lieutenant
May 6, 1793	Robert Armstrong, Jr.	Knox Co. Deputy Sheriff
Nov. 26, 1795	Robert Armstrong	Knox Co. Militia, Ensign
Dec. 15, 1790	William Armstrong	Davidson Co. Militia, Ensign
Feb. 28, 1794	William Armstrong	Hawkins Co. Justice of the Peace
Apr. 11, 194	Martin Ashburn	Knox Co. Militia, Ensign
Nov. 3, 1790	Nathaniel Austin	Hawkins Co. Militia, Captain
Nov. 1, 1790	Waighstill Avery	Licensed to practice law
Oct. 23, 1790	Daniel Bailess	Washington Co. Militia, Ensign
June 10, 1791	William Bailey	Hawkins Co. Militia, Captain
Oct. 23, 1790	Francis Baker	Washington Co. Constable
Jan. 11, 1796	Elisha Baker	Tennessee Constitution Convention
June 16, 1792	Amos Balch	Jefferson Co. Justice of the Peace
Dec. 15, 1790	Samuel Barton	Davidson Co. Justice of the Peace
May 10, 1791	Russell Bean	Washington Co. Deputy Sheriff
June 16, 1792	Hugh Beard	Knox Co. Militia, Second Major
June 16, 1792	Hugh Beard	Knox Co. Calvary, Captain
June 16, 1792	Hugh Beard	Knox Co. Justice of the Peace
Nov. 3, 1790	John Beard	Hawkins Co. Militia, Captain
June 16, 1792	John Beard	Knox Co. Militia, Captain
Feb. 24, 1794	John Beard	Knox Co. Territory Assembly Rep.
Nov. 1, 1790	Samuel Beard	Greene Co. Militia, Captain
Oct. 25, 1790	Andrew Beaty	Sullivan Co. Militia, Captain
Oct. 25, 1790	James Beaty	Sullivan Co. Militia, Ensign
Dec. 15, 1790	George Bell	Tennessee Co. Justice of the Peace
June 10, 1791	William Bell	Hawkins Co. Militia, Ensign
Oct. 25, 1790	Francis Berry	Sullivan Co. Militia, Captain
Nov. 3, 1790	James Berry	Hawkins Co. Justice of the Peace
Jan. 11, 1796	James Berry	Tennessee Constitution Convention
Nov. 3, 1790	Thomas Berry	Hawkins Co. Sheriff

Nov. 3, 1790	Thomas Berry	Hawkins Co. Militia, Captain
Mar. 8, 1791	Thomas Berry	Hawkins Co. Sheriff
Mar. 5, 1792	Thomas Berry	Hawkins Co. Sheriff
June 16, 1792	Thomas Berry	Hawkins Co. Militia, First Major
May 11, 1793	Thomas Berry	Sullivan Co. Justice of the Peace
Sept. 24, 1793	Thomas Berry	Hawkins Co. Militia, Lt. Colonel
Apr. 16, 1794	Thomas Berry	Hawkins Co. Sheriff
Feb. 2, 1795	Thomas Berry	Hawkins Co. Sheriff & 1795 Tax Collector
May 2, 1795	Thomas Berry	Hawkins Co. Sheriff until June 1796 term
Jan. 27, 1796	Thomas Berry	Hawkins Co. Tax Collector for 1796
Oct. 23, 1790	Thomas Biddle	Washington Co. Militia, Captain
Feb. 7, 1795	Abraham Bird	Jefferson Co. Militia, Captain
Oct. 9, 1794	Jesse Bird	Sevier Co. Register
Nov. 3, 1790	Stephen Bird	Hawkins Co. Militia, Ensign
June 16, 1792	Stephen Bird	Knox Co. Militia, Lieutenant
June 16, 1792	Joseph Black	Knox Co. Militia, Captain
Jan. 11, 1796	Joseph Black	Tennessee Constitution Convention
June 16, 1792	William Blackburn	Jefferson Co. Justice of the Peace
Dec. 15, 1790	George Blackmore	Davidson Co. Constable
Dec. 15, 1790	George Blackmore	Mero District Calvary, Captain
Jan. 16, 1795	George D. Blackmore	Mero District Calvary, Second Major
Dec. 15, 1790	William Blackmore	Mero District Calvary, Lieutenant
June 2, 1791	William Blackmore	Mero District Calvary, Captain
Nov. 3, 1790	James Blair	Hawkins Co. Justice of the Peace
Oct. 23, 1790	John Blair	Washington Co. Militia, First Major
Nov. 3, 1790	John Blair	Hawkins Co. Militia, Lt. Colonel
Dec. 5, 1792	John Blair	Washington Co. Militia, Lt. Colonel
Sept. 25, 1794	John Blair	Washington Co. Justice of the Peace
Oct. 25, 1790	Robert Blair	Sullivan Co. Militia, Ensign
Nov. 3, 1790	Robert Blair	Hawkins Co. Militia, Ensign
Oct. 25, 1790	William Blair	Sullivan Co. Militia, Lieutenant
Dec. 15, 1790	Isaac Bledsoe	Sumner Co. Justice of the Peace
Oct. 23, 1790	John Blevins	Washington Co. Militia, Ensign
June 18, 1790	William Blount	Southwest Territory Governor
Jan. 11, 1796	William Blount	Tennessee Constitution Convention, Speaker
July 30, 1796	William Blount	United States Senator, Tennessee
Jan. 10, 1794	Willie Blount	Southwest Territory Notary Public
Apr. 18, 1794	Willie Blount	Licensed to practice law
Oct. 27, 1795	Willie Blount	Licensed to practice law in Superior Courts

Aug. 3, 1795	Andrew Bogle	Blount Co. Justice of the Peace
Apr. 15, 1794	Samuel Bogle	Knox Co. Militia, Ensign
Feb. 3, 1795	Samuel Bogle	Knox Co. Militia, Lieutenant
Aug. 3, 1795	Samuel Bogle	Blount Co. Militia, Ensign
Mar. 7, 1791	Bazil Boran	Tennessee Co. Justice of the Peace
Oct. 25, 1790	Samuel Bouchers	Sullivan Co. Militia, Captain
Oct. 23, 1790	Obadiah Bounds	Washington Co. Militia, Lieutenant
May 10, 1791	Thomas Bounds	Washington Co. Constable
Oct. 23, 1790	Cornelius Bowman	Washington Co. Militia, Captain
May 10, 1791	Cornelius Bowman	Washington Co. Justice of the Peace
June 16, 1792	Robert Boyd	Knox Co. Militia, Ensign
Apr. 15, 1794	Robert Boyd	Knox Co. Militia, Lieutenant
Feb. 3, 1795	Robert Boyd	Knox Co. Militia, Captain
Aug. 3, 1795	Robert Boyd	Blount Co. Militia, Ensign
Dec. 15, 1790	John Boyd Jr.	Davidson Co. Constable
June 10, 1791	Henry Bradford	Mero District Militia, Brigade Major
Oct. 25, 1790	David Bragg	Sullivan Co. Militia, Captain
May 2, 1795	Henry Brazeale	Knox Co. Deputy Sheriff
Oct. 23, 1790	Joseph Bretain	Washington Co. Justice of the Peace
July 14, 1792	Robert Brigance	Sumner Co. Militia, Lieutenant
Oct. 25, 1793	David Brigham	Sullivan Co. Calvary, Cornet
June 16, 1792	Moses Brooks	Knox Co. Militia, Ensign
Jan. 11, 1796	Moses Brooks	Tennessee Constitution Convention
Nov. 1, 1790	William Brotherton	Greene Co. Militia, Lieutenant
Nov. 3, 1790	Alexander Brown	Washington District Calvary, Lieutenant
Nov. 1, 1790	Hugh Brown	Greene Co. Militia, Ensign
Oct. 23, 1790	Jacob Brown	Washington Co. Militia, Captain
Dec. 15, 1790	Thomas Brown	Davidson Co. Militia, Captain
Nov. 1, 1790	Barnabas Brumley	Greene Co. Constable
May 2, 1791	Barnabas Brumley	Greene Co. Constable
Nov. 1, 1790	Thomas Brumley	Greene Co. Constable
May 2, 1791	Thomas Brumley	Greene Co. Constable
Nov. 1, 1790	John Bryan	Greene Co. Militia, Ensign
Oct. 9, 1794	Peter Bryan	Sevier Co. Justice of the Peace
Oct. 9, 1794	Peter Bryan	Sevier Co. Militia, First Major
Jan. 11, 1796	Peter Bryan	Tennessee Constitution Convention
June 16, 1792	Peter Bryants	Jefferson Co. Militia, Captain
Jan. 11, 1796	Thomas Buckenham	Tennessee Constitution Convention
Oct. 23, 1795	Nathaniel Buckingham	Sevier Co. Sheriff until January 1796 term

Jan. 7, 1796	Nathaniel Buckingham	Sevier Co. Deputy Sheriff
Feb. 2, 1795	Thomas Buckingham	Sevier Co. Sheriff & 1795 Tax Collector
May 2, 1795	Thomas Buckingham	Sevier Co. Sheriff to April term 1796
Oct. 9, 1794	Thomas Buckingham Jr.	Sevier Co. Sheriff
Jan. 7, 1796	Thomas Buckingham Jr.	Sevier Co. Sheriff, for one year
Jan. 27, 1796	Thomas Buckingham Jr.	Sevier Co. Tax Collector for 1796
Nov. 3, 1790	James Bunch	Hawkins Co. Militia, Captain
Apr. 26, 1793	John Bunch	Knox Co. Militia, Ensign
Apr. 11, 194	John Bunch	Knox Co. Militia, Captain
Oct. 25, 1790	William Burk	Sullivan Co. Militia, Captain
May 10, 1791	Samuel Burns	Washington Co. Constable
July 14, 1792	John Butler	Sumner Co. Militia, Ensign
July 11, 1795	James Byrnes	Davidson Co. Justice of the Peace
Dec. 15, 1790	Stephen Byrnes	Davidson Co. Militia, Lieutenant
Nov. 25, 1794	Stephen Byrnes	Davidson Co. Militia, Captain
July 6, 1795	Reuben Cage	Sumner Co. Sheriff until July 1796 term
Jan. 27, 1796	Reuben Cage	Sumner Co. Tax Collector for 1796
Dec. 15, 1790	William Cage	Sumner Co. Sheriff
June 2, 1791	William Cage	Sumner Co. Sheriff
July 3, 1792	William Cage	Sumner Co. Sheriff
June 6, 1793	William Cage	Sumner Co. Sheriff
July 9, 1794	William Cage	Sumner Co. Sheriff
Feb. 2, 1795	William Cage	Sumner Co. Sheriff & 1795 Tax Collector
Jan. 17, 1795	Wilson Cage	Mero District Calvary, Lieutenant
Dec. 15, 1790	Jesse Cain	Tennessee Co. Militia, Captain
Sept. 24, 1793	Ballard Caldwell	Hawkins Co. Militia, Ensign
Feb. 28, 1794	Benjamin Caldwell	Hawkins Co. Justice of the Peace
Nov. 3, 1790	David Caldwell	Hawkins Co. Constable
Mar. 8, 1791	David Caldwell	Hawkins Co. Constable
Aug. 4, 1794	David Caldwell	Knox Co. Justice of the Peace
Nov. 3, 1790	Thomas Caldwell	Hawkins Co. Justice of the Peace
June 16, 1792	Thomas Camble	Jefferson Co. Militia, Ensign
June 16, 1792	William Camble	Jefferson Co. Militia, Ensign
June 8, 1790	David Campbell	Southwest Territory Federal Judge
Nov. 3, 1790	David Campbell	Hawkins Co. Militia, Captain
June 16, 1792	David Campbell	Knox Co. Justice of the Peace
June 16, 1792	David Campbell	Knox Co. Militia, Captain
Oct. 23, 1790	John Campbell	Washington Co. Militia, Captain
Nov. 1, 1790	Robert Campbell	Greene Co. Justice of the Peace

Nov. 1, 1790	Robert Campbell	Greene Co. Militia, Captain
Oct. 23, 1790	Solomon Campbell	Washington Co. Militia, Lieutenant
May 2, 1793	William Campbell	Jefferson Co. Militia, Ensign
Dec. 15, 1790	Stephen Cantril	Sumner Co. Militia, Lieutenant
June 15, 1793	Alexander Carmichael	Knox Co. Militia, Lieutenant
Nov. 3, 1790	John Carnes	Hawkins Co. Justice of the Peace
Oct. 23, 1790	Nicholas Carriger	Washington Co. Militia, Lieutenant
Oct. 23, 1790	David Carson	Washington Co. Militia, Lieutenant
June 16, 1792	Robert Carson	Jefferson Co. Militia, Captain
June 6, 1793	John Carter	Washington Co. Justice of the Peace
Sept. 3, 1794	John Carter	Wash. Dist. Clerk & Master Equity Courts
Oct. 23, 1790	Landon Carter	Washington Co. Justice of the Peace
Oct. 23, 1790	Landon Carter	Wash. Co. Militia Commandant, Lt. Col.
Appendix A 6	Landon Carter	Southwest Terr. Affidavits Commissioner
Sept. 30, 1794	Landon Carter	Hamilton District Treasurer
Sept. 30, 1794	Landon Carter	Washington District Treasurer
Jan. 11, 1796	Landon Carter	Tennessee Constitution Convention
Oct. 30, 1790	Matthew Caruthers	Sullivan Co. Constable
Mar. 16, 1791	Matthew Caruthers	Sullivan Co. Constable
Nov. 3, 1790	Samuel Caruthers	Washington District Calvary, Lieutenant
June 14, 1791	Richard Cavet	Sumner Co. Justice of the Peace
June 16, 1792	Thomas Chapman	Knox Co. Register
Jan. 31, 1795	William Childers	Sullivan Co. Militia, Second Major
June 14, 1791	[Blank] Childers	Davidson Co. Militia, Ensign
Oct. 25, 1790	William Childress	Sullivan Co. Militia, Captain
June 10, 1791	Elijah Chisholm	Hawkins Co. Militia, Captain
Nov. 3, 1790	Elijah Chisolm	Hawkins Co. Justice of the Peace
Aug. 1, 1795	James Chisolm	Hawkins Co. Militia, Lieutenant
Oct. 23, 1790	John Chisolm	Washington Co. Justice of the Peace
June 16, 1792	John Chisolm	Knox Co. Justice of the Peace
Oct. 25, 1790	Gilbert Christian	Sullivan Co. Justice of the Peace
Oct. 25, 1790	Gilbert Christian	Sullivan Co. Militia Commandant, Lt. Col.
Oct. 25, 1790	Robert Christian	Sullivan Co. Militia, Captain
Sept. 10, 1792	[Blank] Christmas	Mero District Calvary, Cornet
June 16, 1792	William Churchman	Jefferson Co. Militia, Ensign
July 15, 1795	John Clack	Sevier Co. Justice of the Peace
Jan. 11, 1796	John Clack	Tennessee Constitution Convention
Jan. 11, 1796	Spencer Clack	Tennessee Constitution Convention
Nov. 14, 1795	William C.C. Claiborne	Washington District Militia, Brigade Major

May 22, 1794	William Cole Claiborne	Licensed to practice law, Territory wide
Jan. 11, 1796	William Cole Claiborne	Tennessee Constitution Convention
Dec. 15, 1790	Elisha Clarey	Sumner Co. Militia, Lieutenant
Oct. 23, 1790	John Clark	Washington Co. Militia, Ensign
June 14, 1791	Richard Clark	Davidson Co. Militia, Lieutenant
Oct. 23, 1790	William Cobb	Washington Co. Justice of the Peace
Dec. 15, 1790	John Cochran	Davidson Co. Militia, Ensign
June 14, 1791	John Cochran	Davidson Co. Militia, Lieutenant
Aug. 3, 1795	John Cochran	Blount Co. Militia, Ensign
Aug. 4, 1794	John Cocke	Licensed to practice law
Oct. 24, 1795	John Cocke	Licensed to practice law in Superior Courts
Nov. 3, 1790	William Cocke	Licensed to practice law
Feb. 15, 1791	William Cocke	Washington District Attorney General
Feb. 24, 1794	William Cocke	Territory Assembly Rep., Hawkins Co.
Jan. 11, 1796	William Cocke	Tennessee Constitution Convention
July 30, 1796	William Cocke	United States Senator
Oct. 25, 1790	Elisha Cole	Sullivan Co. Militia, Ensign
Oct. 25, 1790	Joseph Cole	Sullivan Co. Militia, Captain
Mar. 19, 1794	John Collier	Greene Co. Justice of the Peace
Nov. 1, 1790	George Conway	Greene Co. Militia, Captain
May 2, 1795	George Conway	Greene Co. Sheriff & 1795 Tax Collector
Jan. 27, 1796	George Conway	Greene Co. Tax Collector for 1796
May 9, 1793	Joseph Conway	Greene Co. Justice of the Peace
Nov. 1, 1790	Thomas Conway	Greene Co. Militia, Ensign
Nov. 1, 1790	Thomas Conway	Greene Co. Militia, Lieutenant
May 6, 1793	William Conway	Greene Co. Deputy Sheriff
Feb. 2, 1795	William Conway	Greene Co. Sheriff & 1795 Tax Collector
Nov. 27, 1795	William Conway	Washington District Calvary, Second Lt.
Nov. 9, 1790	Elijah Cooper	Washington Co. Stray Master
Nov. 3, 1790	James Cooper	Hawkins Co. Militia, Captain
Nov. 3, 1790	John Cooper	Hawkins Co. Militia, Ensign
Nov. 1, 1790	Stephen Copeland	Greene Co. Militia, Captain
June 16, 1792	Stephen Copeland	Jefferson Co. Militia, Captain
Dec. 15, 1790	William Corbet	Davidson Co. Militia, Ensign
Dec. 15, 1790	John Cordry	Tennessee Co. Militia, Lieutenant
Sept. 15, 1791	John Cordry	Tennessee Co. Militia, Lieutenant
June 16, 1792	James Cosby	Knox Co. Militia, Captain
Dec. 15, 1790	John Couts	Tennessee Co. Militia, Lieutenant
June 16, 1792	Andrew Cowan	Knox Co. Militia, Lieutenant

May 2, 1793	Andrew Cowen	Jefferson Co. Justice of the Peace
Nov. 3, 1790	John Cox	Hawkins Co. Justice of the Peace
Nov. 3, 1790	Thomas Cox	Hawkins Co. Militia, Lieutenant
June 16, 1792	Thomas Cox	Knox Co. Militia, Captain
June 16, 1792	Thomas Cox	Knox Co. Militia, Lieutenant
June 16, 1792	William Cox	Jefferson Co. Justice of the Peace
Nov. 3, 1790	Joseph Crabb	Hawkins Co. Constable
Mar. 8, 1791	Joseph Crabb	Hawkins Co. Constable
Nov. 3, 1790	John Crafford	Hawkins Co. Militia, Captain
June 16, 1792	John Crafford	Knox Co. Militia, Captain
Oct. 25, 1790	Joseph Craft	Sullivan Co. Militia, Ensign
June 16, 1792	David Craig	Knox Co. Justice of the Peace
Oct. 31, 1794	David Craig	Licensed to trade with Indians for horses
Oct. 31, 1794	David Craig	Security for traders with Indians
Aug. 3, 1795	David Craig	Blount Co. Justice of the Peace
Jan. 11, 1796	David Craig	Tennessee Constitution Convention
Jan. 11, 1796	John Crawford	Tennessee Constitution Convention
Oct. 30, 1790	Joseph Crocket	Sullivan Co. Stray Master
Nov. 3, 1790	Jacob Croft	Hawkins Co. Constable
June 16, 1792	James Crosby	Knox Co. Justice of the Peace
Feb. 28, 1794	John Crouch	Washington Co. Justice of the Peace
Nov. 1, 1790	Edmund Crump	Greene Co. Constable
May 2, 1791	Edward Crump	Greene Co. Constable
Dec. 15, 1790	Anthony Crutcher	Tennessee Co. Court Clerk
July 14, 1792	John Cummins	Sumner Co. Militia, Lieutenant
Sept. 20, 1793	James Cunningham	Knox Co. Calvary, Lieutenant
Aug. 3, 1795	James Cunningham	Blount Co. Calvary, Captain
Jan. 27, 1795	James Cunningham	Hamilton District Calvary, First Lt.
June 2, 1791	George Davidson	Mero District Calvary, Cornet
June 13, 1794	Frederick Davis	Davidson Co. Justice of the Peace
Oct. 23, 1790	George Davis	Washington Co. Militia, Ensign
Oct. 30, 1790	James Davis	Sullivan Co. Constable
Mar. 16, 1791	James Davis	Sullivan Co. Constable
June 16, 1792	Wilson Davis	Knox Co. Militia, Ensign
July 11, 1795	John Deaderick	Davidson Co. Justice of the Peace
Oct. 25, 1790	William Delany	Sullivan Co. Justice of the Peace
Oct. 23, 1790	James Denton	Washington Co. Constable
May 10, 1791	James Denton	Washington Co. Constable
Feb. 28, 1794	Henry Dier	Hawkins Co. Militia, Ensign

July 11, 1795	Benjamin Dillard	Washington Co. Justice of the Peace
Aug. 1, 1795	Samuel Doack	Knox Co. Justice of the Peace
June 16, 1792	Reuben Dobin	Jefferson Co. Militia, Lieutenant
June 16, 1792	George Dohorty	Jefferson Co. Justice of the Peace
June 16, 1792	George Dohorty	Jefferson Co. Militia Commandant, Lt. Col.
Feb. 24, 1794	George Dohorty	Territory Assembly Rep., .Jefferson Co.
Jan. 11, 1796	George Dohorty	Tennessee Constitution Convention
June 16, 1792	James Dohorty	Jefferson Co. Militia, Captain
Nov. 1, 1790	James Donaho	Greene Co. Militia, Captain
Mar. 2, 1795	Thomas Donald	Sumner Co. Justice of the Peace
Jan. 23, 1793	William Donaldson	Jefferson Co. Justice of the Peace
Dec. 15, 1790	John Donelson	Davidson Co. Justice of the Peace
June 14, 1791	Samuel Donelson	Davidson Co. Militia, Ensign
Nov. 17, 1794	Samuel Donelson	Licensed to practice law
Dec. 5, 1795	Samuel Donelson	Licensed to practice law in Superior Courts
Nov. 3, 1790	Stockley Donelson	Hawkins Co. Militia Commandant, Lt. Col.
Feb. 26, 1794	Stockley Donelson	Territory Assembly Counsellor Nominee
Aug. 25, 1794	Stockley Donelson	Southwest Territory Assembly Counsellor
Dec. 15, 1790	William Donelson	Davidson Co. Militia, Captain
June 2, 1791	William Donelson	Davidson Co. Militia, Second Major
Oct. 26, 1794	William Donelson	Davidson Co. Militia, Lt. Colonel
Dec. 15, 1790	Edward Douglas	Sumner Co. Justice of the Peace
Dec. 15, 1790	Edward Douglas	Sumner Co. Militia, Second Major
Dec. 15, 1790	Reuben Douglas	Mero District Calvary, Lieutenant
Jan. 16, 1795	Edward Douglass	Sumner Co. Militia, Lt. Colonel
Jan. 11, 1796	Edward Douglass	Tennessee Constitution Convention
Jan. 17, 1795	Reuben Douglass	Mero District Calvary, Captain
Jan. 11, 1796	William Douglass	Tennessee Constitution Convention
Sept. 24, 1793	Pleasant Duke	Hawkins Co. Militia, Captain
Dec. 15, 1790	Martin Duncan	Tennessee Co. Justice of the Peace
Nov. 1, 1790	Ephraim Dunlap	Licensed to practice law
Oct. 25, 1790	Samuel Dunsmore	Sullivan Co. Militia, Ensign
Oct. 25, 1790	Robert Easly	Sullivan Co. Militia, Ensign
Sept. 15, 1791	Archibald Edmiston	Tennessee Co. Militia, Ensign
Sept. 10, 1792	John Edmiston	Davidson Co. Militia, Captain
Dec. 15, 1790	Robert Edmiston	Davidson Co. Justice of the Peace
Mar. 8, 1794	Robert Edmiston	Tennessee Co. Justice of the Peace
Dec. 15, 1790	William Edmiston	Mero District Calvary, Captain
June 2, 1791	William Edmiston	Mero District Calvary, Second Major

Dec. 15, 1790	Alson Edney	Davidson Co. Militia, Ensign
Oct. 30, 1790	Able Edwards	Sullivan Co. Constable
Dec. 15, 1790	John Edwards	Tennessee Co. Militia, Ensign
June 16, 1792	John Ellis	Jefferson Co. Militia, Ensign
Sept. 30, 1794	Robert Eslee	Sullivan Co. Justice of the Peace
Feb. 28, 1794	John Estis	Hawkins Co. Justice of the Peace
June 16, 1792	Andrew Evans	Knox Co. Militia, Ensign
Oct. 9, 1794	Andrew Evans	Sevier Co. Justice of the Peace
Nov. 1, 1790	James Evans	Greene Co. Militia, Captain
June 16, 1792	John Evans	Knox Co. Justice of the Peace
Feb. 7, 1795	Joseph Evans	Hamilton District Calvary, Captain
June 16, 1792	Nathaniel Evans	Knox Co. Calvary, Lieutenant
Jan. 14, 1793	Nathaniel Evans	Knox Co. Calvary, Captain
Feb. 7, 1795	Nathaniel Evans	Jefferson Co. Militia, First Major
Aug. 3, 1795	George Ewin	Blount Co. Justice of the Peace
Aug. 3, 1795	George Ewin	Blount Co. Militia, Captain
Dec. 15, 1790	Andrew Ewing	Davidson Co. Court Clerk
June 16, 1792	George Ewing	Knox Co. Militia, Captain
Dec. 15, 1790	Robert Ewing	Davidson Co. Justice of the Peace
Nov. 3, 1790	George Farragut	Washington District Calvary, Second Major
Mar. 1, 1792	George Farragut	Washington District Muster Master
May 2, 1793	James Ferguson	Jefferson Co. Militia, Ensign
June 16, 1792	Robert Ferguson	Knox Co. Militia, Lieutenant
June 16, 1792	Robert Field	Jefferson Co. Militia, Lieutenant
May 2, 1793	Robert Field	Jefferson Co. Militia, Lieutenant
Nov. 3, 1790	Edward Fields	Hawkins Co. Constable
Nov. 1, 1790	Peter Fine	Greene Co. Militia, Captain
Apr. 16, 1794	John King Fitzgerrald	Jefferson Co. Deputy Sheriff
June 16, 1792	Samuel Flanagan	Knox Co. Militia, Captain
Dec. 15, 1790	James Fleming	Tennessee Co. Militia, Captain
June 16, 1792	Thomas Flippen	Jefferson Co. Militia, Captain
May 2, 1793	Thomas Flippen	Jefferson Co. Militia, Captain
Nov. 3, 1790	Thomas Flipping	Hawkins Co. Militia, Captain
Dec. 15, 1790	James Ford	Tenn. Co. Militia Commandant, Lt. Col.
Feb. 24, 1794	James Ford	Territory Assembly Rep., Tennessee Co.
Jan. 11, 1796	James Ford	Tennessee Constitution Convention
Jan. 11, 1796	William Ford	Tennessee Constitution Convention
June 10, 1791	James Forgey	Hawkins Co. Militia, Lieutenant
June 6, 1793	Elias Fort	Tennessee Co. Justice of the Peace

June 6, 1793	William Fort	Tennessee Co. Justice of the Peace
Feb. 26, 1794	William Fort	Territory Assembly Counsellor Nominee
Dec. 15, 1790	James Frazier	Sumner Co. Militia, Captain
Jan. 17, 1795	James Frazer	Sumner Co. Militia, First Major
May 27, 1794	Samuel Frazier	Greene Co. Justice of the Peace
Jan. 11, 1796	Samuel Frazier	Tennessee Constitution Convention
May 11, 1793	James Gains	Sullivan Co. Justice of the Peace
Jan. 11, 1796	John Galbreath	Tennessee Constitution Convention
Jan. 6, 1794	William Gallahar	Washington Co. Calvary, Cornet
Oct. 25, 1790	Richard Gammon	Sullivan Co. Justice of the Peace
Feb. 26, 1794	Richard Gammon	Territory Assembly Counsellor Nominee
Jan. 11, 1796	Richard Gammon	Tennessee Constitution Convention
Oct. 23, 1790	Thomas Gann	Washington Co. Militia, Lieutenant
Dec. 15, 1790	Argalus Geeter	Davidson Co. Militia, Ensign
June 16, 1792	Bartley Gentry	Jefferson Co. Militia, Lieutenant
June 16, 1792	Hiram Geron	Knox Co. Militia, Ensign
Nov. 3, 1790	John Gibbons	Hawkins Co. Militia, Lieutenant
July 13, 1795	Nicholas Gibbs	Knox Co. Justice of the Peace
Nov. 1, 1790	John Gibson	Greene Co. Militia, Ensign
Jan. 18, 1794	Samuel Gibson	Knox Co. Militia, Adjutant
June 10, 1791	John Gilham	Hawkins Co. Militia, Lieutenant
Nov. 1, 1790	Allen Gillaspie	Greene Co. Militia, Ensign
May 1, 1792	Allen Gillaspie	Washington Co. Deputy Sheriff
May 6, 1793	Allen Gillaspie	Washington Co. Deputy Sheriff
Apr. 16, 1794	Allen Gillaspie	Washington Co. Deputy Sheriff
May 1, 1792	George Gillaspie	Washington Co. Sheriff
May 6, 1793	George Gillaspie	Washington Co. Sheriff
Apr. 16, 1794	George Gillaspie	Washington Co. Sheriff
Feb. 2, 1795	George Gillaspie	Wash. Co. Sheriff & 1795 Tax Collector
May 2, 1795	George Gillaspie	Wash. Co. Sheriff until May 1796 term
Jan. 27, 1796	George Gillaspie	Washington Co. Tax Collector for 1796
Mar. 7, 1791	Thomas Gillaspie	Washington Co. Justice of the Peace
June 16, 1792	Thomas Gillaspie	Knox Co. Militia, Captain
Dec. 15, 1790	William Gillaspie	Davidson Co. Militia, Captain
Mar. 18, 1791	William Gillaspie	Mero District Calvary, Captain
Nov. 3, 1790	Hiram Girin	Hawkins Co. Militia, Ensign
Nov. 1, 1790	Joseph Gist	Greene Co. Militia, Lieutenant
June 16, 1792	Joshua Gist	Jefferson Co. Justice of the Peace
Oct. 9, 1794	Joshua Gist	Sevier Co. Justice of the Peace

Aug. 3, 1795	Samuel Glass	Blount Co. Militia, First Major
Jan. 11, 1796	Samuel Glass	Tennessee Constitution Convention
Dec. 15, 1790	William Glats	Tennessee Co. Militia, Captain
Jan. 4, 1793	George Gordon	Jefferson Co. Militia, Ensign
Nov. 1, 1790	John Gordon	Greene Co. Justice of the Peace
Sept. 10, 1792	John Gordon	Davidson Co. Militia, Lieutenant
Sept. 27, 1794	John Gordon	Hawkins Co. Justice of the Peace
July 11, 1795	John Gordon	Davidson Co. Justice of the Peace
June 6, 1793	Abraham Gormly	Knox Co. Justice of the Peace
Jan. 7, 1796	Thomas Gray	Licensed to practice law, Territory Wide
Feb. 7, 1795	Daniel Green	Hawkins Co. Justice of the Peace
June 16, 1792	Jesse Green	Knox Co. Militia, Ensign
Dec. 15, 1790	Zachariah Green	Mero District Calvary, Cornet
Oct. 31, 1794	James Greenaway	Licensed to trade with Indians for horses
Aug. 3, 1795	James Greenaway	Blount Co. Justice of the Peace
Jan. 11, 1796	James Greenaway	Tennessee Constitution Convention
Jan. 18, 1794	Jesse Greene	Knox Co. Militia, Lieutenant
Oct. 23, 1790	Alexander Greer	Washington Co. Militia, Captain
Dec. 5, 1792	Alexander Greer	Washington Co. Militia, Second Major
Sept. 3, 1794	Alexander Greer	Washington Co. Coroner
Oct. 23, 1790	Andrew Greer	Washington Co. Justice of the Peace
Feb. 7, 1794	David Greer	Licensed to practice law, Territory wide
July 26, 1791	Joseph Greer	Washington Co. Coroner
Jan. 14, 1793	Joseph Greer	Knox Co. Justice of the Peace
Oct. 25, 1790	James Gregg	Sullivan Co. Militia, Captain
Nov. 1, 1790	Samuel Gregg	Greene Co. Militia, Captain
Dec. 15, 1790	George Grims	Davidson Co. Constable
Nov. 1, 1790	John Guess	Greene Co. Justice of the Peace
Nov. 3, 1790	Hugh Gwinn	Hawkins Co. Militia, Lieutenant
June 16, 1792	John Hacket	Knox Co. Justice of the Peace
Oct. 23, 1790	James Hall	Washington Co. Militia, Ensign
Feb. 28, 1794	Nathaniel Hall	Washington Co. Justice of the Peace
Nov. 1, 1790	Samuel Hall	Greene Co. Constable
May 2, 1791	Samuel Hall	Greene Co. Constable
Jan. 1, 1795	William Hall	Sumner Co. Militia, Ensign
July 6, 1795	William Hall	Sumner Co. Calvary, Cornet
Nov. 3, 1790	James Hamilton	Washington District Calvary, Cornet
Dec. 15, 1790	James Hamilton	Sumner Co. Militia, Ensign
Nov. 1, 1790	Joseph Hamilton	Licensed to practice law

Feb. 26, 1791	Joseph Hamilton	Hawkins Co. Attorney and Solicitor
June 16, 1792	Joseph Hamilton	Jefferson Co. Court Clerk
Oct. 25, 1790	Joshua Hamilton	Sullivan Co. Militia, Lieutenant
June 16, 1792	William Hamilton	Knox Co. Justice of the Peace
Mar. 8, 1791	Daniel Hamlin	Hawkins Co. Coroner
Mar. 8, 1791	John Hamlin	Hawkins Co. Constable
Jan. 11, 1796	Samuel Handly	Tennessee Constitution Convention
June 16, 1792	Abraham Hankins	Jefferson Co. Militia, Ensign
June 16, 1792	William Hankins	Knox Co. Militia, Ensign
Sept. 10, 1792	William Hankins	Davidson Co. Militia, Lieutenant
Apr. 26, 1793	William Hankins	Knox Co. Militia, Lieutenant
Jan. 17, 1795	William Hankins	Sumner Co. Militia, Lieutenant
Jan. 17, 1795	Smith Hansborough	Sumner Co. Militia, Captain
Jan. 27, 1796	Nicholas P. Hardeman	Davidson Co. Tax Collector for 1796
Jan. 11, 1796	Thomas Hardeman	Tennessee Constitution Convention
Dec. 15, 1790	Abraham Harden	Tennessee Co. Militia, Ensign
Nov. 1, 1790	Joseph Harden	Greene Co. Justice of the Peace
July 15, 1794	Nicholas P. Hardiman	Davidson Co. Sheriff
Feb. 2, 1795	Nicholas P. Hardiman	Davidson Co. Sheriff & 1795 Tax Collector
July 14, 1795	Nicholas P. Hardiman	Davidson Co. Sheriff until July 1796 term
Sept. 10, 1792	Perkins Hardiman	Davidson Co. Militia, Ensign
Feb. 24, 1794	Joseph Hardin	Territory Assembly Rep., Greene Co.
Nov. 3, 1790	Stephen Hardin	Washington District Calvary, Cornet
Oct. 23, 1790	Michael Harrison	Washington Co. Sheriff
Nov. 3, 1790	Michael Harrison	Washington District Calvary, Captain
Apr. 26, 1793	Solomon Harrison	Knox Co. Militia, Lieutenant
Dec. 15, 1790	David Hay	Davidson Co. Justice of the Peace
Dec. 15, 1790	David Hay	Davidson Co. Militia, Second Major
June 10, 1791	David Hay	Davidson Co. Militia, First Major
Nov. 3, 1790	Mordecai Haygood	Hawkins Co. Constable
Nov. 1, 1790	George Hays	Greene Co. Militia, Captain
Nov. 1, 1790	James Hays	Greene Co. Constable
May 2, 1791	James Hays	Greene Co. Constable
Nov. 1, 1790	Nathaniel Hays	Greene Co. Militia, Lieutenant
Nov. 1, 1790	Robert Hays	Greene Co. Militia, Ensign
Dec. 15, 1790	Robert Hays	Davidson Co. Justice of the Peace
Dec. 15, 1790	Robert Hays	Mero Dist. Calvary Commandant, Lt. Col.
Mar. 1, 1792	Robert Hays	Mero District Militia, Muster Master
Sept. 3, 1794	Andrew Henderson	Jefferson Co. Coroner

Nov. 1, 1790	Daniel Henderson	Greene Co. Constable
May 2, 1791	Daniel Henderson	Greene Co. Constable
Feb. 28, 1794	Nathaniel Henderson	Hawkins Co. Justice of the Peace
Feb. 7, 1795	Robert Henderson	Hamilton District Calvary, Cornet
Nov. 3, 1790	Thomas Henderson	Hawkins Co. Justice of the Peace
Jan. 11, 1796	Thomas Henderson	Tennessee Constitution Convention
Nov. 3, 1790	William Henderson	Hawkins Co. Militia, Lieutenant
June 16, 1792	William Henderson	Jefferson Co. Militia, Lieutenant
Sept. 24, 1793	William Henderson	Hawkins Co. Militia, Lieutenant
Feb. 7, 1795	William Henderson	Hamilton District Calvary, First Lt.
Oct. 23, 1790	Samuel Hendley	Washington Co. Justice of the Peace
Oct. 23, 1790	Samuel Hendley	Washington Co. Militia, Captain
May 10, 1791	Abraham Henry	Washington Co. Constable
Dec. 15, 1790	David Henry	Mero District Calvary, Lieutenant
Mar. 7, 1791	Hugh Henry	Tennessee Co. Justice of the Peace
June 16, 1792	John Henry	Jefferson Co. Militia, Captain
June 16, 1792	Samuel Henry	Knox Co. Militia, Captain
Dec. 15, 1790	Edwin Hickman	Davidson Co. Justice of the Peace
Dec. 15, 1790	Edwin Hickman	Mero District Calvary, First Major
Sept. 15, 1791	Willis Hicks	Tennessee Co. Militia, Ensign
Nov. 1, 1790	James Hill	Greene Co. Militia, Captain
Nov. 1, 1790	Joseph Hinnon	Greene Co. Militia, Ensign
May 6, 1793	Charles Hodge	Jefferson Co. Deputy Sheriff
June 16, 1792	Robert Hodge	Jefferson Co. Deputy Sheriff
Mar. 29, 1794	Charles Hodges	Jefferson Co. Militia, Captain
Mar. 29, 1794	Edmund Hodges	Jefferson Co. Militia, Lieutenant
Jan. 1, 1795	Edward Hogan	Sumner Co. Militia, Ensign
June 10, 1791	James Hoggett	Davidson Co. Justice of the Peace
Dec. 15, 1790	Joseph Hooper	Davidson Co. Militia, Ensign
June 16, 1792	John Horner	Jefferson Co. Militia, Lieutenant
May 10, 1791	George Houce	Washington Co. Constable
Oct. 23, 1790	George House	Washington Co. Constable
June 6, 1793	James Houston	Knox Co. Justice of the Peace
Aug. 3, 1795	James Houston	Blount Co. Militia, Ensign
Jan. 11, 1796	James Houston	Tennessee Constitution Convention
May 6, 1793	Robert Houston	Knox Co. Sheriff
Apr. 16, 1794	Robert Houston	Knox Co. Sheriff
Feb. 2, 1795	Robert Houston	Knox Co. Sheriff & 1795 Tax Collector
May 2, 1795	Robert Houston	Knox Co. Sheriff to April 1796 term

Jan. 27, 1796	Robert Houston	Knox Co. Tax Collector for 1796
Aug. 3, 1795	Samuel Houston	Blount Co. Justice of the Peace
Aug. 3, 1795	Samuel Houston	Blount Co. Militia, Ensign
June 16, 1792	William Houston	Knox Co. Sheriff
June 16, 1792	James Houstone, Jr.	Knox Co. Militia, Ensign
Apr. 26, 1793	James Hubbard	Mounted Infantry Lt., under Maj. Beard
Feb. 7, 1795	James Hubbard	Jefferson Co. Militia, Second Major
Dec. 15, 1790	Zebulon Hubbard	Sumner Co. Militia, Captain
June 16, 1792	John Huest	Jefferson Co. Militia, Ensign
Nov. 3, 1790	John Hunt	Hawkins Co. Militia, Captain
May 2, 1793	John Hurst	Jefferson Co. Militia, Lieutenant
July 8, 1795	John Inman	Jefferson Co. Militia, Captain
May 10, 1791	Robert Irvine	Washington Co. Deputy Sheriff
June 16, 1792	Jeremiah Jack	Knox Co. Justice of the Peace
Dec. 15, 1790	Andrew Jackson	Licensed to practice law, Territory wide
Feb. 15, 1791	Andrew Jackson	Mero District Attorney General
Sept. 10, 1792	Andrew Jackson	Mero District Militia, Judge Advocate
Jan. 11, 1796	Andrew Jackson	Tennessee Constitution Convention
July 30, 1796	Andrew Jackson	United States House of Representatives
Mar. 8, 1791	John Jackson	Hawkins Co. Constable
Mar. 16, 1791	Peter Jackson	Sullivan Co. Constable
Jan. 14, 1793	Thomas Jackson	Hawkins Co. Register
May 30, 1793	Thomas Jackson	Hawkins Co. Justice of the Peace
Oct. 30, 1790	William Jackson	Sullivan Co. Constable
June 16, 1792	William Jackson	Jefferson Co. Justice of the Peace
Oct. 25, 1790	Jacob Job	Sullivan Co. Militia, Ensign
May 2, 1791	William Job	Greene Co. Constable
June 16, 1792	William Job	Jefferson Co. Militia, Captain
June 14, 1791	Henry Johnson	Tennessee Co. Sheriff
June 6, 1793	Henry Johnson	Tennessee Co. Sheriff
May 2, 1791	James Johnson	Greene Co. Constable
Nov. 1, 1790	John Johnson	Greene Co. Militia, Ensign
June 16, 1792	Robert Johnson	Knox Co. Militia, Lieutenant
Dec. 15, 1790	Thomas Johnson	Tennessee Co. Militia, Captain
Sept. 15, 1791	Thomas Johnson	Mero District Calvary, Captain
July 29, 1792	Thomas Johnson	Tennessee Co. Justice of the Peace
June 10, 1791	Thomas Johnson	Tennessee Co. Register
Sept. 12, 1794	Thomas Johnson	Tennessee Co. Militia, First Major
Jan. 11, 1796	Thomas Johnson	Tennessee Constitution Convention

Sept. 30, 1794	Walter Johnson	Sullivan Co. Justice of the Peace
July 29, 1792	William Johnson	Tennessee Co. Justice of the Peace
Nov. 1, 1790	James Johnston	Greene Co. Constable
Nov. 9, 1793	John Jones	Greene Co. Justice of the Peace
Jan. 14, 1793	John Kellams	Knox Co. Calvary, Cornet
Aug. 1, 1795	Daniel Kellum	Hawkins Co. Militia, Ensign
June 16, 1792	Alexander Kelly	Knox Co. Justice of the Peace
June 16, 1792	Alexander Kelly	Knox Co. Militia, Lt. Colonel
Feb. 24, 1794	Alexander Kelly	Territory Assembly Rep., Knox Co.
Aug. 3, 1795	Alexander Kelly	Blount Co. Militia Commandant, Lt. Col.
Oct. 23, 1790	Joshua Kelly	Washington Co. Justice of the Peace
June 16, 1792	Hugh Kelsey	Jefferson Co. Militia, Second Major
Nov. 1, 1790	Daniel Kennedy	Greene Co. Court Clerk
May 10, 1791	Daniel Kennedy	Southwest Terr. Affidavits Commissioner
Dec. 15, 1790	Thomas Kennedy	Davidson Co. Militia, Lieutenant
June 16, 1792	John Kernes	Knox Co. Justice of the Peace
Nov. 1, 1790	Joseph Kersey	Greene Co. Militia, Captain
Nov. 1, 1790	Samuel Kersey	Greene Co. Militia, Lieutenant
Oct. 25, 1790	John Keywood, Jr.	Sullivan Co. Militia, Ensign
Feb. 28, 1794	John Kinchelow	Washington Co. Justice of the Peace
Nov. 3, 1790	James King	Hawkins Co. Militia, Lieutenant
Oct. 31, 1794	James King	Security for traders with Indians
July 11, 1795	James King	Sullivan Co. Justice of the Peace
Oct. 25, 1790	John King	Sullivan Co. Militia, Lieutenant
Nov. 3, 1790	John King	Hawkins Co. Justice of the Peace
Nov. 1, 1790	Johnson King	Greene Co. Militia, Lieutenant
July 14, 1792	Richard King	Sumner Co. Militia, Lieutenant
June 16, 1792	Robert King	Jefferson Co. Militia, Captain
May 2, 1793	Robert King	Jefferson Co. Militia, Captain
Nov. 3, 1790	Thomas King	Washington District Calvary, Lt. Colonel
Oct. 25, 1790	William King	Sullivan Co. Justice of the Peace
Dec. 15, 1790	John Kirkpatrick	Davidson Co. Justice of the Peace
June 16, 1792	Henry Knave	Jefferson Co. Militia, Lieutenant
Dec. 15, 1790	Joseph Kuykendall	Sumner Co. Justice of the Peace
Dec. 15, 1790	Hopkins Lacey	Licensed to practice law
Mar. 15, 1791	Hopkins Lacey	Davidson Co. Attorney and Solicitor
Mar. 15, 1791	Hopkins Lacey	Licensed to practice law, Territory wide
Mar. 1, 1794	Hopkins Lacey	Washington District Attorney General
Aug. 3, 1795	James Woods Lackey	Blount Co. Militia, Second Major

Oct. 23, 1790	Thomas Lackey	Washington Co. Militia, Lieutenant
Feb. 24, 1794	Hopkins Lacy	Southwest Territory Assembly, Clerk
Nov. 1, 1790	James Ladderdale	Greene Co. Militia, Lieutenant
Nov. 1, 1790	William Ladderdale	Greene Co. Militia, Ensign
Nov. 3, 1790	Isaac Lane	Hawkins Co. Justice of the Peace
Nov. 3, 1790	David Larkin	Hawkins Co. Justice of the Peace
Nov. 3, 1790	Thomas Larkin	Hawkins Co. Militia, Lieutenant
Feb. 28, 1794	James Latham	Hawkins Co. Militia, Lieutenant
Jan. 17, 1795	[Blank] Latimer	Sumner Co. Militia, Ensign
Oct. 25, 1790	John Laughlin	Sullivan Co. Militia, Lieutenant
Oct. 23, 1790	John Layman	Washington Co. Militia, Lieutenant
June 16, 1792	James Lea	Jefferson Co. Justice of the Peace
Apr. 29, 1794	James Lea	Jefferson Co. Commissioner of Affidavits
June 16, 1792	Luke Lea	Knox Co. Justice of the Peace
Nov. 1, 1790	John Lee	Greene Co. Justice of the Peace
Nov. 3, 1790	William Lee	Hawkins Co. Militia, Captain
June 16, 1792	Aquila Lenn	Jefferson Co. Militia, Ensign
Oct. 25, 1790	David Lewis	Sullivan Co. Militia, Lieutenant
Sept. 30, 1794	Hugh Lewis	Tennessee Co. Register
Jan. 11, 1796	Joel Lewis	Tennessee Constitution Convention
Oct. 9, 1794	Mordecai Lewis	Sevier Co. Coroner
Oct. 29, 1794	Mordecai Lewis	Sevier Co. Justice of the Peace
June 13, 1794	Seth Lewis	Davidson Co. Justice of the Peace
Nov. 1, 1790	William Lillard	Greene Co. Militia, Captain
June 16, 1792	William Lillard	Jefferson Co. Militia, Captain
Nov. 3, 1790	John Long	Hawkins Co. Justice of the Peace
June 13, 1791	Joseph Long	Washington Co. Cavalry, Lieutenant
May 2, 1793	Benjamin Longacre	Jefferson Co. Militia, Ensign
July 8, 1795	Benjamin Longacre	Jefferson Co. Militia, Ensign
Sept. 27, 1794	Absalom Loony	Hawkins Co. Justice of the Peace
Oct. 25, 1790	David Loony	Sullivan Co. Justice of the Peace
June 16, 1792	Joseph Loony	Knox Co. Justice of the Peace
Dec. 15, 1790	Peter Loony	Sumner Co. Militia, Ensign
July 14, 1792	Peter Loony	Sumner Co. Militia, Captain
Nov. 3, 1790	John Loony Jr.	Hawkins Co. Militia, Ensign
Oct. 23, 1790	James Love	Washington Co. Militia, Captain
Dec. 15, 1790	Josiah Love	Licensed to practice law, Territory wide
Mar. 18, 1791	Josiah Love	Mero District Calvary, Cornet
Oct. 23, 1790	Robert Love	Washington Co. Justice of the Peace

Oct. 23, 1790	Robert Love	Washington Co. Militia, Lt. Colonel
Apr. 17, 1793	John Lowry	Licensed to practice law, Territory wide
Oct. 16, 1794	John Lowry	Licensed to practice law in Superior Courts
Aug. 4, 1794	John Lowry	Licensed to trade with Cherokee Indians
Oct. 31, 1794	John Lowry	Licensed to trade with Indians for horses
Oct. 18, 1794	John Lowry	Sevier Co. Attorney and Solicitor
Aug. 3, 1795	John Lowry	Blount Co. Calvary, First Lieutenant
June 16, 1792	William Lowry	Knox Co. Justice of the Peace
Aug. 3, 1795	William Lowry	Blount Co. Justice of the Peace
Nov. 1, 1790	Joseph Lusk	Greene Co. Militia, Captain
May 9, 1793	Joseph Lusk	Greene Co. Justice of the Peace
Dec. 15, 1790	Adam Lynn	Davidson Co. Justice of the Peace
June 10, 1791	James Maberry	Hawkins Co. Militia, Lieutenant
Feb. 6, 1796	Robert Maclin	Washington Co. Justice of the Peace
Dec. 15, 1790	Archibald Mahan	Tennessee Co. Militia, Ensign
Sept. 15, 1791	Archibald Mahan	Tennessee Co. Militia, Ensign
Feb. 28, 1794	James Mahan	Greene Co. Justice of the Peace
June 16, 1792	John Mahan	Jefferson Co. Militia, Captain
Oct. 9, 1794	John Mahan	Sevier Co. Militia, Captain
Oct. 29, 1790	Stephen Majors	Sullivan Co. Register
Nov. 3, 1790	John Manifee	Hawkins Co. Militia, Captain
June 16, 1792	John Manifee	Knox Co. Justice of the Peace
Nov. 3, 1790	James Mansco	Hawkins Co. Militia, Captain
Dec. 15, 1790	Kasper Mansker	Sumner Co. Militia, Lt. Colonel
Mar. 8, 1791	John Manyfee	Hawkins Co. Justice of the Peace
June 16, 1792	John Manyfee	Knox Co. Militia, Captain
Nov. 3, 1790	Bartlett Marshall	Hawkins Co. Militia, Captain
Dec. 15, 1790	John Marshall	Davidson Co. Militia, Captain
Nov. 3, 1790	John Martin	Hawkins Co. Constable
Mar. 8, 1791	John Martin,Jr.	Hawkins Co. Constable
Mar. 8, 1791	John Martin,Sr.	Hawkins Co. Constable
Oct. 23, 1790	Solomon Massengal	Washington Co. Militia, Ensign
Feb. 7, 1795	William Massingale	Hamilton District Calvary, Second Lt.
Dec. 15, 1790	Thomas Masten	Sumner Co. Justice of the Peace
June 11, 1792	Jeremiah Matthews	Jefferson Co. Court to be held at his house
Nov. 9, 1793	John Maurie	Greene Co. Justice of the Peace
Oct. 23, 1790	Thomas Maxfield	Washington Co. Militia, Captain
Oct. 25, 1790	George Maxwell	Sullivan Co. Justice of the Peace
Mar. 5, 1792	George Maxwell	Sullivan Co. Commissioner of Affidavits

Feb. 28, 1794	George Maxwell	Hawkins Co. Justice of the Peace
June 14, 1791	James Maxwell	Davidson Co. Militia, Captain
Nov. 3, 1790	Richard Maybry	Hawkins Co. Register
Sept. 10, 1792	John Mayes	Davidson Co. Militia, Lieutenant
Nov. 27, 1795	Alexander McAlpin	Washington District Calvary, Cornet
Jan. 23, 1793	John McCallister	Washington Co. Justice of the Peace
Feb. 28, 1794	James McCarthy	Hawkins Co. Justice of the Peace
Jan. 25, 1796	Benjamin McCarty	Hawkins Co. Justice of the Peace
Nov. 3, 1790	William McCarty	Hawkins Co. Militia, Captain
Sept. 24, 1793	William McCarty	Hawkins Co. Militia, Lieutenant
Dec. 15, 1790	Ephraim McClean	Davidson Co. Justice of the Peace
Sept. 10, 1792	Ephraim McClean	Davidson Co. Militia, Ensign
Sept. 10, 1792	George McClean	Davidson Co. Militia, Lieutenant
June 16, 1792	John McCleland	Knox Co. Militia, Ensign
Jan. 27, 1795	John McClellan	Hamilton District Calvary, Captain
Nov. 26, 1795	John McClellan	Knox Co. Justice of the Peace
Feb. 7, 1795	Samuel McClellan	Hamilton District Calvary, Second Lt.
Aug. 2, 1795	Samuel McClellan	Hamilton District Calvary, First Lt.
Jan. 14, 1793	John McClelland	Knox Co. Calvary, Lieutenant
Dec. 15, 1790	Joseph McClewrath	Sumner Co. Militia, Captain
Oct. 23, 1790	William McCloud	Washington Co. Constable
May 10, 1791	William McCloud	Washington Co. Constable
June 16, 1792	Charles McClung	Knox Co. Clerk of the Court
Feb. 7, 1795	Charles McClung	Hamilton District Calvary, Cornet
Aug. 2, 1795	Charles McClung	Hamilton District Calvary, Second Lt.
Jan. 11, 1796	Charles McClung	Tennessee Constitution Convention
Oct. 23, 1790	James McCord	Washington Co. Constable
Feb. 28, 1794	Samuel McCorkle	Sullivan Co. Justice of the Peace
Oct. 25, 1790	William McCormack	Sullivan Co. Deputy Sheriff
Oct. 25, 1790	William McCormack	Sullivan Co. Militia, Captain
June 16, 1792	John McCoulough	Knox Co. Militia, Ensign
May 9, 1793	Abraham McCoy	Jefferson Co. Justice of the Peace
July 8, 1795	Moses McCoy	Jefferson Co. Militia, Lieutenant
Feb. 28, 1794	Charles McCray	Washington Co. Justice of the Peace
June 16, 1792	Thomas McCullock	Knox Co. Justice of the Peace
Aug. 3, 1795	Thomas McCuloch	Blount Co. Justice of the Peace
Apr. 26, 1793	Daniel McDaniel	Knox Co. Militia, Ensign
Nov. 1, 1790	John McDonald	Greene Co. Militia, Lieutenant
July 1, 1792	John McDowell	Surgeon's Mate, Mero Dist. defense Militia

Sept. 23, 1793	John McDowell	Surgeon's Mate for frontier defense troops
Jan. 17, 1795	Joseph McElwrath	Sumner Co. Militia, Second Major
Dec. 15, 1790	David McFaddin	Tennessee Co. Militia, Ensign
Sept. 15, 1791	David McFaddin	Tennessee Co. Militia, Lieutenant
July 8, 1795	George McFarland	Jefferson Co. Militia, Lieutenant
May 2, 1793	James McFarland	Jefferson Co. Militia, Ensign
June 16, 1792	John McFarland	Jefferson Co. Militia, First Major
June 16, 1792	John McFarland	Jefferson Co. Militia, Lieutenant
May 2, 1793	John McFarland	Jefferson Co. Militia, Captain
Nov. 1, 1790	Robert McFarland	Greene Co. Militia, Captain
May 6, 1793	Robert McFarland	Jefferson Co. Sheriff
Apr. 16, 1794	Robert McFarland	Jefferson Co. Sheriff
Jan. 27, 1796	Robert McFarland	Jefferson Co. Tax Collector for 1796
June 16, 1792	Robert McFarlin	Jefferson Co. Sheriff
Feb. 2, 1795	Robert McFarlin	Jefferson Co. Sheriff & 1795 Tax Collector
June 16, 1792	Samuel McGahe	Knox Co. Militia, Captain
June 14, 1791	John McGaugh	Davidson Co. Militia, Ensign
Oct. 9, 1794	Samuel McGaughey	Sevier Co. Militia, Second major
June 10, 1791	William McGehe	Hawkins Co. Militia, Lieutenant
Aug. 4, 1794	Barclay McGhee	Licensed to trade with Cherokee Indians
Oct. 31, 1794	Barclay McGhee	Licensed to trade with Indians for horses
June 16, 1792	Robert McGill	Jefferson Co. Militia, Lieutenant
Nov. 1, 1790	Alexander McGinty	Licensed to practice law
Feb. 18, 1791	Alexander McGinty	Licensed to practice law, Territory wide
June 16, 1792	John McKain	Knox Co. Militia, Lieutenant
Dec. 15, 1790	James McKean, Jr.	Sumner Co. Militia, Captain
Jan. 18, 1795	John McKee	Licensed to practice law
Aug. 3, 1795	John McKee	Blount Co. Clerk
Aug. 3, 1795	John McKee	Blount Co. Militia, Lt. Colonel
June 16, 1792	Alexander McLaughlin	Jefferson Co. Militia, Ensign
Oct. 25, 1790	Abraham McLellan	Sullivan Co. Justice of the Peace
Oct. 25, 1790	John McLellen	Sullivan Co. Militia, Ensign
Apr. 26, 1793	John McMahan	Mounted Infantry Ensign under Maj. Beard
Nov. 3, 1790	Joseph McMinn	Hawkins Co. Militia, Lieutenant
June 10, 1791	Joseph McMinn	Hawkins Co. Militia, Captain
June 16, 1792	Joseph McMinn	Hawkins Co. Militia, Second Major
Nov. 19, 1792	Joseph McMinn	Hawkins Co. Justice of the Peace
Sept. 24, 1793	Joseph McMinn	Hawkins Co. Militia, First Major
Feb. 24, 1794	Joseph McMinn	Territory Assembly Rep., Hawkins Co.

Jan. 11, 1796	Joseph McMinn	Tennessee Constitution Convention
June 16, 1792	John McNab	Jefferson Co. Justice of the Peace
June 16, 1792	John McNab	Jefferson Co. Militia, Lt. Colonel
Feb. 28, 1794	William McNab	Washington Co. Justice of the Peace
Mar. 5, 1792	Andrew McNairy	Mero District Clerk of the Superior Court
June 8, 1790	John McNairy	Southwest Territory Federal Judge
Jan. 11, 1796	John McNairy	Tennessee Constitution Convention
Oct. 23, 1790	Peter McNamer	Washington Co. Deputy Sheriff
June 16, 1792	Geroge McNutt	Knox Co. Justice of the Peace
Oct. 23, 1795	Isaac McNutt	Licensed to practice law, county courts
Oct. 23, 1790	Samuel McQueen	Washington Co. Militia, Captain
June 16, 1792	James McQuiston	Jefferson Co. Militia, Ensign
July 8, 1795	James McQueston	Jefferson Co. Militia, Lieutenant
Dec. 15, 1790	James Mears	Davidson Co. Justice of the Peace
Dec. 15, 1790	James Mears	Davidson Co. Stray Master
Dec. 15, 1790	William Mears	Davidson Co. Militia, Lieutenant
June 16, 1792	Adam Meek	Jefferson Co. Justice of the Peace
Feb. 26, 1794	Adam Meek	Territory Assembly Counsellor Nominee
Mar. 8, 1791	William Meek	Hawkins Co. Constable
Oct. 23, 1790	John Melvin	Washington Co. Militia, Lieutenant
June 16, 1792	James Menasea	Jefferson Co. Militia, Captain
Dec. 15, 1790	Benjamin Menees	Tennessee Co. Justice of the Peace
Oct. 25, 1790	Nicholas Mercer	Sullivan Co. Militia, Lieutenant
June 6, 1793	Charles Miles	Tennessee Co. Justice of the Peace
Nov. 3, 1790	James Miles	Hawkins Co. Militia, Captain
Sept. 12, 1794	Richard Miles	Tennessee Co. Militia, Lt. Colonel
June 6, 1793	William Miles	Tennessee Co. Justice of the Peace
July 14, 1795	William Miles	Tennessee Co. Militia, Second Major
Oct. 23, 1790	John Miligan	Washington Co. Justice of the Peace
Oct. 23, 1790	John Miligan	Washington Co. Militia, Captain
June 16, 1792	Thomas Millegan	Knox Co. Militia, Lieutenant
Nov. 1, 1790	Alen Miller	Greene Co. Militia, Lieutenant
June 16, 1792	Thomas Milligan	Knox Co. Calvary, Cornet
Mar. 8, 1791	Edward Mitchel	Hawkins Co. Deputy Sheriff
June 10, 1791	Edward Mitchel	Hawkins Co. Militia, Ensign
Feb. 28, 1794	Edward Mitchel	Hawkins Co. Militia, Captain
Nov. 19, 1792	Mark Mitchel	Hawkins Co. Justice of the Peace
Nov. 3, 1790	Richard Mitchel	Hawkins Co. Court Clerk
Jan. 11, 1796	Richard Mitchel	Tennessee Constitution Convention

Feb. 27, 1794	Samuel Mitchel	Licensed to practice law, Territory wide
Sept. 3, 1794	Richard Mitchell	Hawkins Co. Stray Master
Dec. 15, 1790	Thomas Molloy	Davidson Co. Justice of the Peace
Dec. 15, 1790	Thomas Molloy	Davidson Co. Register
Mar. 7, 1791	John Montgomery	Tennessee Co. Justice of the Peace
June 5, 1794	James Moore	Knox Co. Justice of the Peace
Feb. 28, 1794	William Moorland	Washington Co. Justice of the Peace
Nov. 9, 1793	Adonijah Morgan	Greene Co. Justice of the Peace
Dec. 15, 1790	John Morgan	Sumner Co. Militia, Captain
Dec. 15, 1790	Joseph Morgan	Sumner Co. Militia, Ensign
July 14, 1792	Joseph Morgan	Sumner Co. Militia, Lieutenant
Oct. 23, 1790	Joseph Morrison	Washington Co. Militia, Lieutenant
Oct. 30, 1790	David Motley	Sullivan Co. Constable
Dec. 15, 1790	James Cole Mountflorence	Licensed to practice law, Territory wide
Mar. 7, 1791	James Cole Mountflorence	Mero District Notary Public
Oct. 9, 1794	Alexander Mountgomery	Sevier Co. Stray Master
Jan. 26, 1794	James Mountgomery	Washington Co. Justice of the Peace
June 16, 1792	James Moyars	Jefferson Co. Militia, Lieutenant
July 8, 1795	James Moyars	Jefferson Co. Militia, Lieutenant
Nov. 1, 1790	John Moyer	Greene Co. Militia, Ensign
Dec. 15, 1790	James Mulherin	Davidson Co. Justice of the Peace
Dec. 15, 1790	Thomas Murray	Davidson Co. Militia, Captain
July 9, 1795	Thomas Murry	Davidson Co. Militia, First Major
Dec. 15, 1790	William Nash	Davidson Co. Militia, Lieutenant
June 3, 1791	William Nash	Sullivan Co. Justice of the Peace
June 14, 1791	William Nash	Davidson Co. Militia, Captain
Sept. 27, 1794	Alexander Nelson	Hawkins Co. Justice of the Peace
May 9, 1793	Hugh Nelson	Greene Co. Justice of the Peace
June 16, 1792	Jesse Nelson	Jefferson Co. Militia, Lieutenant
Dec. 15, 1790	Robert Nelson	Mero District Calvary, Captain
Mar. 7, 1791	Robert Nelson	Tennessee Co. Justice of the Peace
July 11, 1795	William Nelson	Washington Co. Justice of the Peace
Dec. 15, 1790	George Nevil	Tennessee Co. Justice of the Peace
Dec. 15, 1790	Joseph Nevil	Tennessee Co. Sheriff
Mar. 8, 1791	William Nevil	Hawkins Co. Constable
July 15, 1794	Joseph Nevill	Tennessee Co. Sheriff
Feb. 2, 1795	Joseph Nevill	Tenn. Co. Sheriff & 1795 Tax Collector
July 14, 1795	Joseph Nevill	Tennessee Co. Sheriff, until July term 1796
Jan. 27, 1796	Joseph B. Nevill	Tennessee Co. Tax Collector for 1796

June 16, 1792	Samuel Newell	Knox Co. Justice of the Peace
Oct. 9, 1794	Samuel Newell	Sevier Co. Justice of the Peace
Oct. 9, 1794	Samuel Newell	Sevier Co. Militia, Lt. Colonel
Nov. 1, 1790	Cornelius Newman	Greene Co. Constable
Nov. 1, 1790	Cornelius Newman	Greene Co. Militia, Lieutenant
May 2, 1791	Cornelius Newman	Greene Co. Constable
Nov. 1, 1790	John Newman	Greene Co. Justice of the Peace
Nov. 1, 1790	John Newman	Greene Co. Stray Master
June 14, 1791	John Nichols	Davidson Co. Justice of the Peace
Sept. 24, 1793	John Nichols	Hawkins Co. Militia, Lieutenant
July 14, 1792	Ezekial Norris	Sumner Co. Militia, Captain
Oct. 23, 1790	George North	Washington Co. Militia, Captain
Dec. 15, 1790	David Nowland	Davidson Co. Militia, Ensign
Oct. 23, 1790	Henry Oldham	Washington Co. Militia, Ensign
Apr. 18,1794	James Ore	Hawkins Co. Militia, Second Major
Oct. 31, 1794	James Ore	Security for traders with Indians
Nov. 1, 1790	Alexander Outlaw	Greene Co. Justice of the Peace
June 16, 1792	Alexander Outlaw	Jefferson Co. Justice of the Peace
Jan. 11, 1796	Alexander Outlaw	Tennessee Constitution Convention
Dec. 15, 1790	John Overton	Licensed to practice law, Territory wide
May 13, 1795	John Overton	Territory Supervisor of Revenue
Dec. 15, 1790	Philip Parchment	Tennessee Co. Militia, Lieutenant
Sept. 15, 1791	Philip Parchment	Tennessee Co. Militia, Captain
Dec. 15, 1790	Charles Parker	Davidson Co. Militia, Captain
Oct. 30, 1790	Charles Parker	Sullivan Co. Constable
Oct. 24, 1795	Isham Allen Parker	Licensed to practice law, county courts
Sept. 10, 1792	John Parks	Davidson Co. Militia, Captain
Nov. 1, 1790	James Patterson	Greene Co. Justice of the Peace
Nov. 3, 1790	John Patterson	Hawkins Co. Militia, Captain
June 16, 1792	Robert Patterson	Knox Co. Militia, Ensign
Apr. 26, 1793	Robert Patterson	Knox Co. Militia, Ensign
Nov. 26, 1795	Robert Patterson	Knox Co. Militia, Lieutenant
Dec. 15, 1790	Thomas Patton	Sumner Co. Militia, Lieutenant
July 14, 1792	Thomas Patton	Sumner Co. Militia, Captain
Sept. 25, 1794	Jesse Payne	Washington Co. Justice of the Peace
Nov. 3, 1790	John Payne	Hawkins Co. Deputy Sheriff
Mar. 8, 1791	John Payne	Hawkins Co. Deputy Sheriff
Nov. 3, 1790	William Payne	Hawkins Co. Justice of the Peace
Nov. 19, 1792	Adam Peck	Jefferson Co. Stray Master

Oct. 25, 1790	William Pemberton	Sullivan Co. Militia, Captain
Dec. 15, 1790	Jacob Pennington	Tennessee Co. Justice of the Peace
Dec. 15, 1790	Jacob Pennington	Tennessee Co. Militia, First Major
June 16, 1792	Nicholas Perkins	Jefferson Co. Justice of the Peace
June 16, 1792	Nicholas Perkins	Jefferson Co. Militia, Captain
Jan. 27, 1796	Nicholas Perkins	Davidson Co. Tax Collector for 1796
June 10, 1791	Nicholas T. Perkins	Hawkins Co. Militia, Ensign
Nov. 3, 1790	Joseph Perrin	Hawkins Co. Justice of the Peace
Oct. 25, 1790	David Perry	Sullivan Co. Justice of the Peace
Nov. 3, 1790	William Peyne, Sr.	Hawkins Co. Militia, Lieutenant
July 29, 1792	Isaac Philips	Tennessee Co. Justice of the Peace
Dec. 15, 1790	John Philips	Tennessee Co. Justice of the Peace
Dec. 15, 1790	John Phillips	Tennessee Co. Stray Master
Dec. 15, 1790	Ezekiel Polk	Tennessee Co. Justice of the Peace
Oct. 29, 1794	Robert Pollock	Sevier Co. Justice of the Peace
Dec. 15, 1790	William Porter	Davidson Co. Militia, Lieutenant
Dec. 15, 1790	Francis Prince	Tennessee Co. Justice of the Peace
July 16, 1792	Robert Prince	Tennessee Co. Sheriff
Jan. 11, 1796	Robert Prince	Tennessee Constitution Convention
June 8, 1792	William Prince	Tennessee Co. Coroner
Jan. 11, 1796	William Prince	Tennessee Constitution Convention
Feb. 28, 1794	William Pursley	Washington Co. Justice of the Peace
Aug. 3, 1795	Henry Ragan	Blount Co. Militia, Ensign
Aug. 3, 1795	John Ragan	Blount Co. Militia, Ensign
Nov. 9, 1793	William Ragan	Greene Co. Justice of the Peace
Aug. 3, 1795	William Ragan	Blount Co. Militia, Lieutenant
Feb. 3, 1795	Henry Ragen	Knox Co. Militia, Ensign
Dec. 15, 1790	John Rains	Davidson Co. Militia, Captain
Nov. 3, 1790	Francis Alex.Ramsey	Washington District Calvary, First Major
Nov. 3, 1790	Francis Alex.Ramsey	Washington District Superior Court Clerk
Mar. 7, 1791	Francis Alex.Ramsey	Washington District Notary Public
Mar. 29, 1796	Francis Alex.Ramsey	Tennessee Senate Clerk
Dec. 15, 1790	Josiah Ramsey	Tennessee Co. Militia, Second Major
Nov. 1, 1790	David Rankin	Greene Co. Justice of the Peace
Jan. 11, 1796	William Rankin	Tennessee Constitution Convention
Nov. 1, 1790	Asahel Rawlings	Greene Co. Coroner
Nov. 1, 1790	Asahel Rawlings	Greene Co. Justice of the Peace
June 6, 1793	Phelps Read	Hawkins Co. Justice of the Peace
Nov. 3, 1790	William Read	Hawkins Co. Justice of the Peace

Nov. 9, 1793	William Reagan	Greene Co. Justice of the Peace
Apr. 26, 1793	John Reagin	Knox Co. Militia, Ensign
June 16, 1792	William Reagin	Knox Co. Militia, Lieutenant
Nov. 1, 1790	John Reagon	Greene Co. Militia, Ensign
Dec. 15, 1790	William Reasons	Mero District Calvary, Cornet
Sept. 29, 1794	William Reasons	Tennessee Co. Militia, Adjutant
Nov. 1, 1790	James Rees	Licensed to practice law
Nov. 9, 1790	James Rees	Washington Co. Attorney and Solicitor
Nov. 3, 1790	Samuel Regs	Hawkins Co. Militia, Lieutenant
July 15, 1795	William Renno	Sevier Co. Justice of the Peace
June 16, 1792	Joseph Renny	Jefferson Co. Militia, Lieutenant
June 16, 1792	Archibald Rhea	Knox Co. Militia, Lieutenant
Nov. 1, 1790	John Rhea	Licensed to practice law
Nov. 22, 1790	John Rhea	Licensed to practice law, Territory wide
Nov. 22, 1790	John Rhea	Sullivan Co. Attorney and Solicitor
Jan. 11, 1796	John Rhea	Tennessee Constitution Convention
Oct. 25, 1790	Matthew Rhea	Sullivan Co. Militia, First Major
Oct. 25, 1790	Matthew Rhea	Sullivan Co. Court Clerk
Jan. 31, 1795	Matthew Rhea	Sullivan Co. Militia, Lt. Colonel
June 16, 1792	Robert Rhea	Knox Co. Militia, Lieutenant
Aug. 3, 1795	Robert Rhea	Blount Co. Coroner
Aug. 3, 1795	Robert Rhea	Blount Co. Militia, Ensign
May 11, 1793	William Rhea	Sullivan Co. Justice of the Peace
Dec. 15, 1790	Joel Rice	Davidson Co. Justice of the Peace
Nov. 1, 1790	James Richardson	Greene Co. Sheriff
Nov. 3, 1790	James Richardson	Washington District Calvary, Captain
May 2, 1791	James Richardson	Greene Co. Sheriff
May 1, 1792	James Richardson	Greene Co. Sheriff
May 6, 1793	James Richardson	Greene Co. Sheriff
Apr. 16, 1794	James Richardson	Greene Co. Sheriff
June 16, 1792	William Richardson	Jefferson Co. Militia, Ensign
May 2, 1793	William Richardson	Jefferson Co. Militia, Lieutenant
Nov. 1, 1790	Archibald Roan	Greene Co. Attorney and Solicitor
Nov. 1, 1790	Archibald Roan	Licensed to practice law
Jan. 11, 1796	Archibald Roan	Tennessee Constitution Convention
Aug. 2, 1795	Henry Roberts	Hamilton District Calvary, Cornet
Dec. 15, 1790	Isaac Roberts	Davidson Co. Militia, First Major
June 10, 1791	Isaac Roberts	Davidson Co. Militia, Lt. Colonel
Oct. 27, 1792	Isaac Roberts	Davidson Co. Mil. Commandant, Lt. Col.

Oct. 23, 1790	Charles Robertson	Washington Co. Justice of the Peace
May 10, 1791	Charles Robertson	Washington Co. Sheriff
Dec. 15, 1790	Elijah Robertson	Davidson Co. Justice of the Peace
Dec. 15, 1790	Elijah Robertson	Davidson Co. Militia, Lt. Colonel
June 2, 1791	Elijah Robertson	Davidson Co. Mil. Commandant, Lt. Col.
Dec. 15, 1790	James Robertson	Davidson Co. Justice of the Peace
Dec. 15, 1790	James Robertson	Davidson Co. Mil. Commandant, Lt. Col.
Feb. 23, 1791	James Robertson	Commissioned Lt. General by Congress
June 2, 1791	James Robertson	Mero District Commander, Lt. General
Jan. 11, 1796	James Robertson	Tennessee Constitution Convention
Dec. 15, 1790	Jonathan F. Robertson	Mero District Calvary, Cornet
June 2, 1791	Jonathan F. Robertson	Mero District Calvary, Lieutenant
Nov. 1, 1790	David Robinson	Greene Co. Militia, Lieutenant
June 16, 1792	James Roddye	Jefferson Co. Justice of the Peace
Jan. 11, 1796	James Roddye	Tennessee Constitution Convention
July 8, 1795	George Rogers	Jefferson Co. Militia, Ensign
Apr. 26, 1793	Jeremiah Rogers	Knox Co. Militia, Ensign
Oct. 23, 1790	Joseph Rogers	Washington Co. Militia, Ensign
Nov. 19, 1792	Joseph Rogers	Hawkins Co. Justice of the Peace
Oct. 23, 1790	Moses Rogers	Washington Co. Militia, Lieutenant
Dec. 15, 1790	James Ross	Davidson Co. Justice of the Peace
Oct. 11, 1793	George Roulstone	Knox Co. Commissioner of Affidavits
Aug. 25, 1794	George Roulstone	Territory Assembly, Council Clerk
Dec. 15, 1790	John Rule	Sumner Co. Militia, Ensign
Nov. 3, 1790	Andrew Russell	Wash. Dist. Equity Courts Clerk & Master
Nov. 1, 1790	David Russell	Greene Co. Justice of the Peace
Feb. 26, 1794	David Russell	Territory Assembly Counsellor Nominee
Feb. 26, 1794	Griffith Rutherford	Territory Assembly Counsellor Nominee
Aug. 25, 1794	Griffith Rutherford	Southwest Territory Assembly Counsellor
Oct. 25, 1790	George Rutledge	Sullivan Co. Sheriff
Oct. 25, 1790	George Rutledge	Sullivan Co. Militia, Second Major
Mar. 16, 1791	George Rutledge	Sullivan Co. Sheriff
Feb. 24, 1794	George Rutledge	Territory Assembly Rep., Sullivan Co.
Jan. 31, 1795	George Rutledge	Sullivan Co. Justice of the Peace
Jan. 31, 1795	George Rutledge	Sullivan Co. Militia, First Major
Jan. 11, 1796	George Rutledge	Tennessee Constitution Convention
Nov. 1, 1790	James Rutledge	Greene Co. Constable
May 2, 1791	James Rutledge	Greene Co. Constable
Oct. 25, 1790	Robert Rutledge	Sullivan Co. Deputy Sheriff

Oct. 25, 1790	Robert Rutledge	Sullivan Co. Militia, Lieutenant
Mar. 16, 1791	Robert Rutledge	Sullivan Co. Deputy Sheriff
June 10, 1791	Samuel Samples	Hawkins Co. Militia, Captain
June 16, 1792	Samuel Samples	Knox Co. Militia, Captain
Nov. 3, 1790	John Saunders	Hawkins Co. Militia, Ensign
Nov. 3, 1790	John Sayers	Hawkins Co. Militia, Second Major
June 16, 1792	John Sayers	Knox Co. Justice of the Peace
June 16, 1792	John Sayers	Knox Co. Militia, First Major
Oct. 23, 1790	James Scott	Washington Co. Militia, Lieutenant
June 16, 1792	James Scott	Knox Co. Militia, Lieutenant
Aug. 3, 1795	James Scott	Blount Co. Justice of the Peace
Aug. 3, 1795	James Scott	Blount Co. Militia, Ensign
Oct. 25, 1790	John Scott	Sullivan Co. Justice of the Peace
Oct. 25, 1790	John Scott	Sullivan Co. Militia, Lt. Colonel
Apr. 25, 1792	John Scott	Sullivan Co. Sheriff
Mar. 1, 1794	John Scott	Sullivan Co. Sheriff
Jan. 31, 1795	John Scott	Sullivan Co. Militia Commandant, Lt. Col.
Feb. 2, 1795	John Scott	Sullivan Co. Sheriff & 1795 Tax Collector
Dec. 15, 1790	Bennet Searcy	Sumner Co. Attorney and Solicitor
Dec. 15, 1790	Bennet Searcy	Tennessee Co. Attorney and Solicitor
June 3, 1791	Bennet Searcy	Mero Dist. Equity Courts Clerk & Master
Dec. 10, 1794	Bennet Searcy	Licensed to practice law
June 16, 1792	Patrick Selvedge	Jefferson Co. Militia, Ensign
Nov. 1, 1790	William Senate	Greene Co. Deputy Sheriff
Nov. 9, 1790	James Sevier	Washington Co. Court Clerk
Oct. 23, 1790	John Sevier, Sr.	Washington Co. Justice of the Peace
Feb. 23, 1791	John Sevier, Sr.	Commissioned Lt. General by Congress
June 2, 1791	John Sevier, Sr.	Washington Dist. Commander, Lt. General
Feb. 26, 1794	John Sevier, Sr.	Territory Assembly Counsellor Nominee
Aug. 25, 1794	John Sevier, Sr.	Southwest Territory Assembly Counsellor
Mar. .30, 1796	John Sevier, Sr.	Elected Governor of Tennessee
Sept. 6, 1794	John Sevier, Jr.	Washington Co. Attorney and Solicitor
Sept. 7, 1794	John Sevier, Jr.	Licensed to practice law, Territory wide
Dec. 15, 1790	John Shannon	Davidson Co. Militia, Captain
Oct. 26, 1794	John Shannon	Davidson Co. Militia, Second Major
Dec. 15, 1790	Joseph Shannon	Davidson Co. Militia, Ensign
Dec. 15, 1790	Samuel Shannon	Davidson Co. Coroner
Oct. 25, 1790	Anthony Sharp	Sullivan Co. Militia, Ensign
Dec. 15, 1790	Anthony Sharp	Sumner Co. Justice of the Peace

Dec. 15, 1790	Anthony Sharp	Sumner Co. Militia, First Major
Dec. 15, 1790	William Shaw	Davidson Co. Militia, Lieutenant
Dec. 15, 1790	David Shelby	Sumner Co. Court Clerk
Jan. 11, 1796	David Shelby	Tennessee Constitution Convention
May 2, 1795	Isaac Shelby	Sullivan Co. Sheriff to March term 1796
Jan. 27, 1796	Isaac Shelby	Sullivan Co. Tax Collector for 1796
Oct. 25, 1790	John Shelby	Sullivan Co. Justice of the Peace
Jan. 11, 1796	John Shelby, Jr.	Tennessee Constitution Convention
June 16, 1792	William Shield	Jefferson Co. Militia, Lieutenant
Oct. 30, 1794	John Shields	Greene Co. Attorney and Solicitor
May 2, 1793	William Shields	Jefferson Co. Militia, Captain
Sept. 24, 1793	John Sims	Hawkins Co. Militia, Ensign
Aug. 1, 1795	John Sims	Hawkins Co. Militia, Captain
Aug. 3, 1795	Littlepage Sims	Blount Co. Sheriff
Jan. 27, 1796	Littlepage Sims	Blount Co. Tax Collector for 1796
June 10, 1791	Parish Sims	Hawkins Co. Militia, Ensign
Oct. 25, 1790	William Simson	Sullivan Co. Militia, Lieutenant
June 16, 1792	John Singleton	Knox Co. Militia, Captain
Aug. 3, 1795	John Singleton	Blount Co. Militia, Ensign
Dec. 15, 1790	Joseph Sitgreaves	Licensed to practice law
Dec. 15, 1790	Joseph Sitgreaves	Mero Dist. Equity Courts Clerk & Master
Oct. 25, 1790	William Skillern	Sullivan Co. Militia, Lieutenant
Nov. 1, 1790	John Slaughter	Greene Co. Militia, Lieutenant
June 16, 1792	Abraham Slover	Jefferson Co. Militia, Lieutenant
Nov. 1, 1790	William Small	Greene Co. Constable
Oct. 25, 1790	Solomon Smalling	Sullivan Co. Militia, Captain
Dec. 15, 1790	William Smeathers	Tennessee Co. Constable
June 8, 1790	Daniel Smith	Southwest Territory Secretary
Jan. 11, 1796	Daniel Smith	Tennessee Constitution Convention
Oct. 25, 1790	Daniel Smith	Sullivan Co. Militia, Ensign
Dec. 15, 1790	David Smith	Davidson Co. Militia, Captain
Sept. 10, 1792	David Smith	Mero District Calvary, Lieutenant
Oct. 23, 1790	Edward Smith	Washington Co. Justice of the Peace
Dec. 15, 1790	Ezekiel Smith	Davidson Co. Militia, Captain
May 10, 1791	Jacob Smith	Washington Co. Constable
June 14, 1791	John Smith	Davidson Co. Militia, Ensign
Nov. 3, 1790	Samuel Smith	Hawkins Co. Militia, Lieutenant
June 3, 1791	Samuel Smith	Sullivan Co. Justice of the Peace
June 13, 1794	Thomas Smith	Davidson Co. Justice of the Peace

June 16, 1792	Thomas Snoddy	Jefferson Co. Militia, Ensign
May 2, 1793	Thomas Snoddy	Jefferson Co. Justice of the Peace
Dec. 15, 1790	William Snoddy	Sumner Co. Militia, Ensign
Jan. 17, 1795	William Snoddy	Sumner Co. Militia, Captain
Oct. 25, 1790	William Snodgrass	Sullivan Co. Militia, Lieutenant
Dec. 15, 1790	Charles Snyder	Davidson Co. Militia, Lieutenant
June 15, 1793	John Somerville	Knox Co. Militia, Ensign
Oct. 31, 1794	John Somerville	Security for traders with Indians
Feb. 28, 1794	John Spurgin	Sullivan Co. Justice of the Peace
Nov. 3, 1790	William Standafer	Hawkins Co. Militia, Lieutenant
June 16, 1792	William Standaford	Knox Co. Militia, Lieutenant
Nov. 1, 1790	Ninian Steel	Greene Co. Militia, Captain
Oct. 23, 1790	William Stephenson	Washington Co. Register
Oct. 30, 1790	Edward Sterling	Sullivan Co. Constable
June 16, 1792	James Sterling	Knox Co. Militia, Ensign
Apr. 25, 1792	John Sterling	Hawkins Co. Militia, Ensign
Oct. 23, 1790	James Stewart	Washington Co. Justice of the Peace
Nov. 1, 1790	James Stinson	Greene Co. Deputy Sheriff
May 2, 1791	James Stinson	Greene Co. Deputy Sheriff
June 15, 1793	James Stinson	Greene Co. Register
Nov. 27, 1795	James Stinson	Washington District Calvary, Captain
Nov. 3, 1790	John Stone	Washington District Calvary, Lieutenant
Nov. 22, 1790	John Stone	Greene Co. Register
June 6, 1793	John Stone	Knox Co. Militia, Lieutenant
June 15, 1793	John Stone	Knox Co. Militia, Captain
Oct. 23, 1790	William Stone	Washington Co. Militia, Captain
Oct. 23, 1790	John Strain	Washington Co. Justice of the Peace
Jan. 11, 1796	James Stuart	Tennessee Constitution Convention
Mar. 29, 1796	James Stuart	Tennessee House Speaker
Dec. 15, 1790	Simon Sugg	Davidson Co. Constable
Nov. 3, 1790	Samuel Summer	Washington District Calvary, Cornet
Oct. 23, 1790	William Swiney	Washington Co. Militia, Ensign
Nov. 1, 1790	Edward Tate	Greene Co. Militia, Captain
Dec. 15, 1790	Howell Tatum	Licensed to practice law, Territory wide
Oct. 27, 1792	Howell Tatum	Davidson Co. Militia, Lt. Colonel
Sept. 27, 1794	Howell Tatum	Mero District Treasurer
June 10, 1791	Joseph Taylor	Hawkins Co. Militia, Ensign
Oct. 23, 1790	Leroy Taylor	Washington Co. Militia, Second Major
Dec. 5, 1792	Leroy Taylor	Washington Co. Militia, First Major

Feb. 24, 1794	Leroy Taylor	Territory Assembly Rep., Washington Co.
Jan. 11, 1796	Leroy Taylor	Tennessee Constitution Convention
Nov. 21, 1793	Nathaniel Taylor	Washington Co. Justice of the Peace
Feb. 26, 1794	Permenas Taylor	Territory Assembly Counsellor Nominee
Aug. 25, 1794	Permenas Taylor	Southwest Territory Assembly Counsellor
Feb. 7, 1795	Parmenas Taylor	Jefferson Co. Militia, Commandant, Lt. Col.
Aug. 3, 1795	George Tedford	Blount Co. Militia, Ensign
Aug. 3, 1795	Joseph Tedford	Blount Co. Militia, Ensign
June 16, 1792	Joseph Tedfore	Knox Co. Militia, Captain
Nov. 27, 1795	John Temple	Washington District Calvary, First Lt.
Nov. 9, 1793	Thomas Temple	Greene Co. Justice of the Peace
Dec. 15, 1791	Jesse Terry	Washington Co. Constable
Nov. 19, 1792	Reuben Thornton	Washington Co. Justice of the Peace
Feb. 24, 1794	John Tipton	Territory Assembly Rep., Washington Co.
Jan. 11, 1796	John Tipton	Tennessee Constitution Convention
Oct. 23, 1790	Jonathan Tipton	Washington Co. Militia, Ensign
June 16, 1792	Joshua Tipton	Jefferson Co. Militia, Lieutenant
Dec. 15, 1790	Isaac Titsworth	Tennessee Co. Militia, Lt. Colonel
Nov. 3, 1790	John Toole	Hawkins Co. Militia, Lieutenant
Aug. 3, 1795	John Tremble	Blount Co. Justice of the Peace
Sept. 15, 1791	Alexander Trowsdale	Tennessee Co. Militia, Lieutenant
Oct. 23, 1790	Jonathan Tully	Washington Co. Militia, Captain
Nov. 1, 1790	John Umphry	Greene Co. Justice of the Peace
June 3, 1791	John Vance	Sullivan Co. Justice of the Peace
Oct. 9, 1794	Joseph Vance	Sevier Co. Justice of the Peace
Oct. 23, 1790	John Vantrees	Washington Co. Militia, Ensign
Nov. 1, 1790	Elijah Venteh	Greene Co. Militia, Ensign
Oct. 25, 1790	George Vincent	Sullivan Co. Justice of the Peace
Oct. 23, 1790	David Waggoner	Washington Co. Militia, Lieutenant
Nov. 1, 1790	John Waggoner	Greene Co. Militia, Ensign
Nov. 19, 1792	Mattias Waggoner	Washington Co. Justice of the Peace
June 14, 1791	James Waldrop	Hawkins Co. Militia, Ensign
Dec. 15, 1790	Alexander Walker	Davidson Co. Militia, Lieutenant
June 14, 1791	Alexander Walker	Davidson Co. Militia, Captain
Nov. 1, 1790	Anderson Walker	Greene Co. Militia, Captain
Nov. 1, 1790	Daniel Walker	Greene Co. Militia, Lieutenant
May 2, 1793	Deans Walker	Jefferson Co. Militia, Lieutenant
Mar. 18, 1791	George Walker	Mero District Calvary, Lieutenant
July 8, 1795	James Walker	Jefferson Co. Militia, Lieutenant

June 16, 1792	Jesse Wallace	Knox Co. Militia, Ensign
Nov. 28, 1795	Jesse Wallace	Hamilton District Calvary, Cornet
Aug. 3, 1795	Joel Wallace	Blount Co. Militia, Ensign
Oct. 25, 1790	Joseph Wallace	Sullivan Co. Justice of the Peace
Aug. 4, 1794	Matthew Wallace	Licensed to trade with Cherokee Indians
Aug. 3, 1795	Matthew Wallace	Blount Co. Calvary, Second Lieutenant
Aug. 3, 1795	Matthew Wallace	Blount Co. Justice of the Peace
June 16, 1792	William Wallace	Knox Co. Justice of the Peace
Aug. 3, 1795	William Wallace	Blount Co. Justice of the Peace
Aug. 3, 1795	William Wallace	Blount Co. Register
Nov. 3, 1790	James Walling	Hawkins Co. Militia, Lieutenant
Dec. 15, 1790	Isaac Walton	Sumner Co. Coroner
Dec. 26, 1794	Isaac Walton	Sumner Co. Militia, Lieutenant
Jan. 11, 1796	Isaac Walton	Tennessee Constitution Convention
Dec. 15, 1790	William Walton	Sumner Co. Justice of the Peace
June 16, 1792	Alexander Ward	Jefferson Co. Militia, Captain
Oct. 23, 1790	William Ward	Washington Co. Constable
May 10, 1791	William Ward	Washington Co. Constable
Dec. 15, 1790	Robert Weakly	Davidson Co. Justice of the Peace
June 10, 1791	Robert Weakly	Mero Dist. Mil.. Brigade Inspector, Lt. Col.
June 16, 1792	Samuel Wear	Jefferson Co. Justice of the Peace
Feb. 24, 1794	Samuel Wear	Territory Assembly Rep., Jefferson Co.
Oct. 9, 1794	Samuel Wear	Sevier Co. Clerk
Oct. 9, 1794	Samuel Wear	Sevier Co. Militia Commandant, Lt. Col.
Jan. 11, 1796	Samuel Wear	Tennessee Constitution Convention
Oct. 25, 1790	Jacob Weaver	Sullivan Co. Militia, Lieutenant
Nov. 3, 1790	George Webb	Washington District Calvary, Cornet
Mar. 16, 1791	George Webb	Sullivan Co. Constable
Nov. 3, 1790	Moses Webb	Washington District Calvary, Captain
Mar. 8, 1794	Haden Wells	Tennessee Co. Justice of the Peace
Oct. 25, 1790	Isaac White	Sullivan Co. Militia, Lieutenant
Nov. 3, 1790	James White	Hawkins Co. Justice of the Peace
Nov. 3, 1790	James White	Hawkins Co. Militia, First Major
Dec. 15, 1790	James White	Licensed to practice law, Territory wide
June 16, 1792	James White	Knox Co. Justice of the Peace
June 16, 1792	James White	Knox Co. Militia Commandant, Lt. Col.
Jan. 11, 1796	James White	Tennessee Constitution Convention
Feb. 24, 1794	Dr. James White	Territory Assembly Rep., Davidson Co.
Dec. 15, 1790	John White	Sumner Co. Militia, Lieutenant

Oct. 23, 1790	Richard White	Washington Co. Justice of the Peace
Nov. 1, 1790	William White	Greene Co. Militia, Captain
Dec. 26, 1794	James Whitsitt	Sumner Co. Militia, Ensign
June 16, 1792	James Whitsun	Jefferson Co. Militia, Ensign
Oct. 23, 1790	John Wier	Washington Co. Justice of the Peace
Nov. 1, 1790	John Wier	Greene Co. Justice of the Peace
Dec. 15, 1790	John Wilcox	Tennessee Co. Militia, Lieutenant
Oct. 9, 1794	George Wilcoxon	Sevier Co. Justice of the Peace
Oct. 23, 1790	James Wiley	Washington Co. Militia, Captain
Oct. 23, 1790	Edmond Williams	Washington Co. Justice of the Peace
Oct. 23, 1790	George Williams	Washington Co. Deputy Sheriff
Oct. 23, 1790	George Williams	Washington Co. Militia, Captain
Dec. 20, 1791	George Williams	Washington Co. Ranger and Stray Master
Sept. 24, 1793	James Williams	Hawkins Co. Militia, Lieutenant
Feb. 28, 1794	John Williams	Sullivan Co. Justice of the Peace
Jan. 17, 1795	John Williams	Sumner Co. Militia, Lieutenant
July 8, 1795	John Williams	Jefferson Co. Militia, Ensign
July 14, 1795	Oliver Williams	Davidson Co. Deputy Sheriff
Dec. 15, 1790	Samson Williams	Davidson Co. Sheriff
July 10, 1792	Samson Williams	Davidson Co. Sheriff
June 6, 1793	Samson Williams	Davidson Co. Sheriff
June 13, 1794	Samson Williams	Davidson Co. Justice of the Peace
Nov. 3, 1790	Samuel Williams	Washington District Calvary, Lieutenant
Mar. 29, 1796	Thomas Williams	Tennessee House Clerk
Sept. 10, 1792	John Williamson	Davidson Co. Militia, Captain
Dec. 15, 1790	David Willson	Sumner Co. Justice of the Peace
Nov. 1, 1790	William Willson	Greene Co. Justice of the Peace
June 16, 1792	Adam Wilson	Jefferson Co. Militia, Captain
Oct. 9, 1794	Adam Wilson	Sevier Co. Militia, Captain
Feb. 24, 1794	David Wilson	Territory Assembly Rep., Sumner co.
Feb. 24, 1794	David Wilson	Territory Assembly, House Speaker
Sept. 27, 1794	David Wilson	Sumner Co. Register
Nov. 1, 1790	James Wilson	Greene Co. Justice of the Peace
Dec. 15, 1790	James Wilson	Sumner Co. Stray Master
July 14, 1792	James Wilson	Sumner Co. Militia, Ensign
Feb. 6, 1795	James Wilson	Jefferson Co. Justice of the Peace
Nov. 1, 1790	John Wilson	Greene Co. Militia, Captain
Apr. 16, 1794	John Wilson	Jefferson Co. Deputy Sheriff
May 2, 1795	John Wilson	Jefferson Co. Deputy Sheriff until May 1796

June 16, 1792	Joseph Wilson	Jefferson Co. Justice of the Peace
Oct. 9, 1794	Joseph Wilson	Sevier Co. Justice of the Peace
Aug. 19, 1794	Robert Wilson	Licensed to trade with Cherokee Indians
Oct. 31, 1794	Robert Wilson	Licensed to trade with Indians for horses
Nov. 3, 1790	Samuel Wilson	Hawkins Co. Stray Master
Nov. 9, 1793	Samuel Wilson	Greene Co. Justice of the Peace
Nov. 1, 1790	William Wilson	Greene Co. Militia, Ensign
July 11, 1795	William Wilson	Greene Co. Justice of the Peace
Dec. 15, 1790	George Winchester	Sumner Co. Justice of the Peace
Dec. 15, 1790	George Winchester	Sumner Co. Register
Dec. 15, 1790	George Winchester	Mero District Calvary, Second Major
June 14, 1791	George Winchester	Mero District Calvary, First Major
Dec. 15, 1790	James Winchester	Sumner Co. Justice of the Peace
Dec. 15, 1790	James Winchester	Sumner Co. Militia Commandant, Lt. Col.
Feb. 26, 1794	James Winchester	Territory Assembly Counsellor Nominee
Aug. 25, 1794	James Winchester	Southwest Territory Assembly Counsellor
Mar. 29, 1796	James Winchester	Tennessee Senate Speaker
June 16, 1792	William Winten	Jefferson Co. Militia, Ensign
June 16, 1792	Elijah With	Jefferson Co. Militia, Captain
Nov. 1, 1790	Elijah Witt	Greene Co. Militia, Lieutenant
Sept. 24, 1793	John Wood	Hawkins Co. Militia, Ensign
June 10, 1791	Thomas Woodward	Hawkins Co. Militia, Lieutenant
June 16, 1792	Thomas Woodward	Knox Co. Militia, Lieutenant
Nov. 9, 1793	John Yancey	Sullivan Co. Justice of the Peace
Oct. 25, 1790	Robert Yancy	Sullivan Co. Militia, Ensign
Dec. 15, 1790	James Yates	Sumner Co. Militia, Lieutenant
Oct. 23, 1790	Solomon Yeager	Washington Co. Militia, Lieutenant
Nov. 3, 1790	John Young	Washington District Calvary, Captain
Mar. 16, 1793	John Young	Sumner Co. Militia, Captain
Feb. 28, 1794	Joseph Young	Washington Co. Justice of the Peace

Time Line of Events 1774 - 1796

1774 ◆Dec. 16, 1773 Boston Tea Party.

1775 ◆Sept. 6, 1774 First Continental Congress convenes to develop a united response to England's closing of Boston Port.

◆May 10, 1775 Second Continental Congress meets.

1776

◆July 4, 1776 Declaration of Independence is signed.

1777

1778 ◆Nov. 15, 1777 Watauga Association becomes Washington County, N. C.

1779

1780 ◆Dec. 22, 1779 Robertson & Donaldson lead settlers to Cumberland valley.

1781 ◆Oct. 7, 1780 Overmountain men rout British at Battle of Kings Mountain.

1782 ◆Oct. 19, 1781 Cornwallis surrenders to Washington at Yorktown, VA.

1783

◆Apr. 18, 1783 Davidson Co. North Carolina cut from Washington County.

◆Sept. 3, 1783 Revolutionary War ends with Treaty of Paris.

1784

◆Apr. 23, 1784 Congress passes Northwest Ordinance to govern the West.

1785 ◆Dec. 14, 1784 State of Franklin begins.

1786-
◆Fall of 1785 Hopewell Treaty between Congress and the Southern Indians.

1787-
◆Feb. 21, 1787 Congress calls a convention to revise Articles of Confederation.

1788-
◆Sept. 17, 1787 Delegates unanimously propose a new Federal Constitution.

◆June 21, 1788 New United States Constitution becomes law of the land.

1789-
◆Apr. 30, 1789 George Washington inaugurated President of United States.
◆July 14, 1789 Peasants storm the Bastille and start the French Revolution.

1790-◆Dec. 12, 1789 North Carolina Conditionally Cedes its Western Land to U. S.
◆Apr. 2, 1790 Congress accepts North Carolina's Ceded Western land.
◆June 8, 1790 Washington appoints Blount Gov. of Southwest Territory.

1791-
◆Oct. 23, 1790 Gov. Blount begins control of Territory at Jonesborough.

1792-
◆Nov. 11, 1791 Holston Treaty with Cherokee Indians signed.

◆Aug. 7-11, 1792 Blount & Pickens meet Choctaws & Chickasaws at Nashville.
◆Sept. 15, 1792 Cherokee & Creek Tribes declare war on United States.

1793-

1794-
◆Oct. 19, 1793 Blount calls for election of first Territory Assembly.
◆Feb. 26, 1794 Southwest Territory 1st Legislature meets at Knoxville.

1795-
◆Sept. 17, 1794 Major Ore sacks Cherokee towns Nickajack & Running Water.

1796-◆Jan. 11, 1796 Tennessee Constitution Convention meets at Knoxville.

◆**June 6, 1796 The United States admits Tennessee as the 16th. State.**

1797-

References

1. "Territorial Papers of the United States," Vol. IV, as compiled by Clarence E. Carter.

2. "The Blount Journal, 1791-1796" A journal of the proceedings of William Blount Esquire, Governor in and over the Territory of the United States of America South of the river Ohio. Published by The Tennessee Historical Commission.

3. The "Knoxville Gazette 1791-1797," at the McClung Library, Knoxville, Tennessee.

4. "William Blount," by William H, Masterson, published by the Louisiana State University Press, 1954.

5. "John Sevier, Pioneer of the Old South," by Carl Driver.

6. "Andrew Jackson and Early Tennessee History, II," by S. G Heiskell.

7. "The Tennessee Constitution of 1796: A Product of the Old West," by John D. Burnhart.

8. 'The Tennessee," by Donald Davidson.